Seven Championship-Tested Basketball Offenses

Harry L. "Mike" Harkins

Parker Publishing Company, Inc
West Nyack, New York

Previous books by the author:

Tempo-Control Basketball

Successful Team Techniques in Basketball

Library of Congress Cataloging in Publication Data

Harkins, Harry L
    Seven championship-tested basketball offenses.

    Includes index.
    1. Basketball--Offense. I. Title.
GV889.H35   796.32'32   76-2365
ISBN 0-13-806794-5

Printed in the United States of America

To my mother, Mrs. Georgann Harkins,
and her determination, after being widowed at an early age,
to go out and work to keep her family together
and her children in school.

WHAT THESE
TITLE-TESTED ATTACKS
CAN DO FOR YOU

During the sixteen years I have coached at Eastern Montana College, the Yellowjackets have won twelve Frontier Conference crowns, participated in fourteen N.A.I.A. District 5 Tournaments and won ten of them, played in the N.A.I.A. Tourney at Kansas City ten times, won three Frontier Conference Tournaments, and won two Christmas Tournaments.

These teams have used the fast break, but have always featured a pattern-type offense. In general, the scoring has been well balanced between the players. Even so, we have had twelve players make honorable mention N.A.I.A. All-American, one make second team, and Roy McPipe was named first team N.A.I.A. All-American and second team small college All-American.

Aside from being blessed with talented players over the years, the major key to our success has been the fact that we have selected offenses that allowed us to utilize the strengths of our players and cover up their weaknesses. The offenses have been composed of functional basic plays that many times have been incorporated into continuities.

This book deals with these offensive team techniques. Individual fundamentals are included only within the context of the offense being covered. It is a book for coaches who are seeking new perspectives in offensive basketball.

A full treatment is given to each of the seven offenses in terms of: (1) how they operate against man-to-man defenses, (2) auxiliary plays that may be added to give depth to the offense or meet a particular situation, (3) how the offense may be run against zone defenses, and (4) how to teach the offense, which involves personnel requirements, coaching techniques, and drills.

The seven offenses are:

(1) *The Four-Man Passing Game*.
The author feels this offense will eventually take its place alongside the two greatest offensive team techniques—the Shuffle and the Reverse Action.

(2) *The Passing Game Shuffle*.
An offense that combines the Passing Game and the Shuffle.

(3) *The Post-Oriented Stack Offense*.
For the team with two pivot men that lacks the strong guard to play a one-guard offense.

(4) *The High-Post Wall Offense*.
An offense for the team that lacks a big pivot man.

(5) *The Multi-Option Continuity*.
An offshoot of the Reverse Action Offense with a new approach.

(6) *The Headhunter Shuffle*.
An offense to utilize high-scoring forwards.

(7) *The Stack and Shuffle Continuity*.
An offense that allows a team to run a continuity that incorporates the basic Stack and the Shuffle.

This book gives you seven possible new team approaches to offensive basketball. Considerations are given to: how to combat overplay, removing the sagger, utilizing your personnel, continuity, defensive balance, adapting to zone defenses, and offensive rebounding. If your team's offense is sputtering or you feel the teams in your league know what your players will do before they do it, here are seven new offensive pathways to championship basketball.

Harry L. "Mike" Harkins

Acknowledgments

Special tribute goes to my wife, Grace, for the hours of typing (and her ability to decipher my handwritten manuscript) and for her meticulous efforts on the diagrams.

Grateful appreciation is also expressed to the sources of my basketball knowledge, including:
> Russ Estey and Mike Krino, my high school coaches.
> Russ Beichly and Red Cochrane, my college coaches.
> The players who have played on my teams.
> And the publishers of *The Coaching Clinic*, *Scholastic Coach*, *Coach and Athlete*, and *Athletic Journal*.

A final note of thanks goes to my number one fan (and granddaughter) Shellee Ann Harkins.

Contents

WHAT THESE TITLE-TESTED ATTACKS CAN DO FOR YOU   7

1   THE FOUR-MAN PASSING GAME   15

The Four-Man Passing Game Versus Man-to-Man   15
    The Basic Movement   16
    Basic Movement Rules   16
    The Pivot Man   21
The Four-Man Passing Game Auxiliary Plays   24
    The Quick-Cut Play   24
    The Dribble-Chase Rule   25
    The Second-Guard-Through Play   26
    The Backdoor Play   26
    The Double-Inside Screen   28
    The Stack   30
    The Post-Opposite Play   30
    The Forward-Across Play   31
    The Exchange-Switch Play   32
    The Over-the-Top Play   32
Passing Game Special Continuities   33
    A Reverse-Action-Type Continuity   34
    A Slashing-Type Continuity   35
    A Double-Post-Stack Passing Game Continuity   37
    A Shuffle-Type Action   39
    The Double-Cross Continuity   40
Using the Passing Game Against Zone Defenses   41
    Splitting the Defensive Perimeter   42

Cutting Through the Zone   44
Overloading and Overshifting   44
Rotating the Zone Players   47
Screening the Zone   49
Passing and Cutting Tempo   50
Teaching the Passing Game Offense   50
Personnel   50
Coaching Points   50
Drills to Teach the Passing Game   51
Three-Man Shadow Drill   51
Shadow Drill from the Side Position   54
Shadow Drill from the Corner Position   55
Three-on-Three (Live)   56

2   THE PASSING GAME SHUFFLE   57

The Passing Game Shuffle Versus Man-to-Man   57
The Pattern Set Move   57
The Basic Shuffle   59
Other Methods of Starting the Passing Game Shuffle   61
Auxiliary Plays for the Passing Game Shuffle   64
The Backdoor   64
The Second-Guard-Through Play   66
The Sagger Play   67
The Passing Game Shuffle Versus the Zone Defense   69
Splitting the Zone   69
Utilizing the Overload Triangles   70
Screening the Zone   71
Cutting Through the Zone   72
Teaching the Passing Game Shuffle   73
Coaching Points   73
The Pattern Set Phase   74
The Shuffle Phase   75
Other Options   76
Drills to Teach the Passing Game Shuffle   78
The Screen-and-Roll Drill   78

The Offside Screen-and-Roll Drill   79
The California Drill   80
The Strongside Recognition Drill   81
Progressive Sequence of Offensive Drills   83

3   A POST-ORIENTED STACK OFFENSE   85

The Post-Oriented Stack Versus Man-to-Man   85
     Weakside Action   85
     Strongside Action   89
Post-Oriented Stack Offense Auxiliary Plays   90
     The Wall Play   90
     The Wall Play Outside Cut   91
     The Backdoor Play   92
The Post-Oriented Stack Offense Versus the Zone Defense   93
     Weakside Action   93
     Strongside Action   97
Teaching the Post-Oriented Stack Offense   98
     Coaching Points   98
     Weakside Plays   98
     Strongside Action   103
Drills to Teach the Post-Oriented Stack   103
     The Stack Drill   103
     The Cross Drill   103
     The Basic Plays Drill   103

4   THE HIGH-POST WALL OFFENSE   107

The High-Post Wall Versus Man-to-Man   107
     The Inside Cut   107
     The Outside Cut   108
     The Cross Play   110
High-Post Wall Auxiliary Plays   111
     Kas's Play   111
     The Forward Fake   112

11

The Corner-Reverse Play   113
The Three-in-a-Row Play   116
The Post-Opposite Play   118
The Double-Cut Series   119
The Shuffle Phase   123
Utilizing the High-Post Wall Offense Versus Zone Defenses   128
Splitting the Zone   128
The Inside-Cut Play   131
The Outside-Cut Play   134
The Cross Play   137
Teaching the High-Post Wall Offense   138
Personnel   138
Coaching Points   138
The Inside-Cut Play   139
The Outside Cut   140
The Cross Play   143
Drills to Teach the High-Post Wall Offense   143
The Breakdown Drill   143
The Recognition Drill   143
The Three-Times-Around Drill   145
The Isolation Drill   145

5   THE MULTI-OPTION CONTINUITY   147

The Multi-Option Continuity Versus Man-to-Man   147
Players' Rules   150
The Split Rule   151
Multi-Option Continuity Auxiliary Plays   153
The Cross-Court Lob Play   153
The Corner Play   155
The Wall Play   156
The Multi-Option Continuity Versus Zone Defenses   158
Rotating Front   158
Forward Options   159
Guard Options   161

Teaching the Multi-Option Continuity   161
    Personnel   162
    Coaching Points   163
    Cutting Off the Post Man   163
    The Moving Screen   164
    The Guards' Crossing Action   165
Drills to Teach the Multi-Option Continuity   165
    One-on-One in the Post   165
    Forwards' Two-on-Two   166
    The California Drill   167

6   THE HEADHUNTER SHUFFLE   169

The Headhunter Shuffle Versus Man-to-Man   169
    The Inside Headhunter Play   169
    The Outside Headhunter Play   172
    The Post Play   173
The Headhunter Shuffle Auxiliary Plays   175
    The Post Play   175
    The Lob Play   175
    The Lob Play from the Outside Cut   176
    The Shallow Cut Play   177
    The Forward Low Play   178
The Headhunter Shuffle Versus Zone Defenses   178
    The Basic Play   178
    Catching the Overshift   179
    Switching the Overload   180
    Utilizing Triangles   181
Teaching the Headhunter Shuffle   181
    Personnel   181
    Coaching Points   182
    The Inside Headhunter Play   182
    The Outside Headhunter Play   185
    The Post Play   185
    Drills to Teach the Headhunter Shuffle   186
    High-Post Jump Shot   186

The Split Drill   186
The Shuffle Phase Drill   190

7 THE STACK AND SHUFFLE CONTINUITY   191

The Stack and Shuffle Continuity Versus Man-to-Man   191
The Basic Stack Play   191
The Basic Shuffle Play   193
Conversion   194
Auxiliary Plays for the Stack and Shuffle Continuity   196
The High-Post Screen   196
The Backdoor Play   198
The Low-Post Split   199
The Wing Clear (from the Double Stack)   201
The Stack and Shuffle Continuity Versus Zone Defenses   202
The Stack Phase   202
The Shuffle Phase   204
Teaching the Stack and Shuffle Continuity   205
Personnel   205
Coaching Points   206
The Stack Phase   206
The Shuffle Phase   207
Drills to Teach the Stack and Shuffle Continuity   208
The Recognition Drill   208
The Skeleton Drill   208
The California Drill   208
The Defensive Balance Drill   209

INDEX   211

1

The Four-Man Passing Game

In recent years an offense called the Passing Game has been developed in California. The concept of the offense was originated by Robert "Duck" Dowell of Pepperdine College. It is now used by numerous teams and in many variations.

THE FOUR-MAN PASSING GAME VERSUS MAN-TO-MAN

The Passing Game is the type of offense in which the players are not governed by stereotyped patterns, but rather by a few simple rules. It has the attribute of being very simple to teach and learn, and yet it presents the defense with a myriad of problems. Even though it is not a rigid, regimented offense, it still avoids the chaos that frequently plagues a free-lance type of game.

Another feature of this offense is its adaptability. Although its basic use is against man-to-man defenses, it also may be adapted to work against zone defenses, used as a control or stall game, and run versus half- or full-court pressure defenses. Since the basketball teams of today often vary their defenses several times in a given game, this type of offense is probably a preview of the offenses of the future.

Although the Passing Game may be run with or without a pivot man, the following treatment will concern itself with the four-man movement plus a pivot man.

The Basic Movement

A coach is always seeking two types of movement from his players:

First, when a player has received the ball, he should attempt to "put a move on" his opponent. The Passing Game gives each player receiving a pass this opportunity because he:

(1) is coming off an offside screen.
(2) has made a change of direction before coming to the ball.
(3) is moving toward the ball.
(4) has room to work because the passer clears to the opposite side of the court.

The second type of movement coaches seek concerns movement away from the ball. This involves:

(1) keeping his defensive man moving away from the teammate with the ball who is attempting to score.
(2) being ready to receive a pass when the man with the ball has completed his move.

Basic Movement Rules

The passing game meets both of these basic movement functions with three rules:

Pass the Ball and Move Away from Your Pass. While you are doing this, screen for your teammates and continue to the offside baseline.

This usually involves three types of situations:

(1) A guard passes to the other guard and screens opposite for the forward on his own side of the court. (See Diagram 1-1)

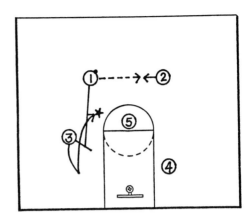

DIAGRAM 1-1

The passing guard then goes to the baseline and out.

(2) A guard passes to the forward on his side, screens opposite for the other guard and continues to the offside baseline. (Diagram 1-2)

This is the preferable move because it gets the ball to an ideal one-on-one position (the forward in the corner).

(3) The third situation is a forward-to-guard pass. After the pass the forward then cuts back to the baseline and out sharply for a return pass if needed. (Diagram 1-3)

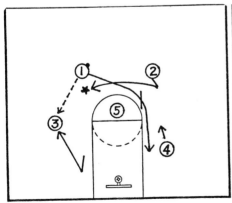

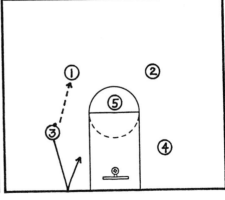

DIAGRAM 1-2   DIAGRAM 1-3

17

A clever forward can sometimes work a backdoor play on his defender in this situation.

NOTE: It is a functional practice to thoroughly move the defense with these three options and wait until all four players involved in the basic movement have been to the baseline before taking a shot. This is especially true at the beginning of a game or second-half period.

The Second Rule Involves the Utilization of the Pivot Man. With any pass to the pivot man, the forwards and guards exchange positions. In effect, this results in a split play on the ball side and an offside exchange on the other. In Diagram 1-4, the ball is passed to the pivot man by a guard. Since a guard made the pass, the guards move first, go inside, and are the screeners.

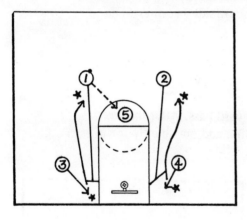

DIAGRAM 1-4

The forwards make a move toward the basket, which may result in a backdoor of their defender, and come off the screen set by the guard on their side. The pivot man (5) looks first for the possible backdoor, then for the forwards coming out or the guards inside.

When a forward makes the pass to the pivot man, the forwards go inside and are the screeners. The guards change direction and then cut to the forward position. The first option is for the post man (5) to pass to either of the guards inside. If a switch occurs, one of the forwards may be open. (Diagram 1-5)

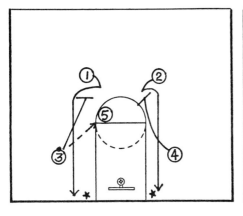

DIAGRAM 1-5

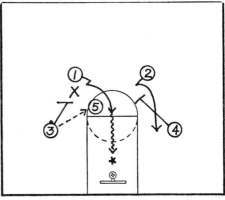

DIAGRAM 1-6

If the guard's defender does not respect the change of direction, the guard may backdoor him and go down the middle. (Diagram 1-6)

The Third Rule Covers Cutting to the Basket. During the basic movement described in the first rule, an offensive man will often find he has beaten his defender to the extent that he has a clear cut to the basket. We tell our players that any time you can get your head and shoulders past the defender, you may cut to the basket. If the cut is unsuccessful, the cutter goes to either corner, although we prefer him to go to the offside corner. (Diagrams 1-7 and 1-8)

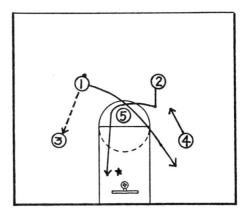

DIAGRAM 1-7

19

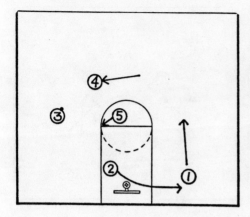

DIAGRAM 1-8

As shown in Diagrams 1-7 and 1-8, player (2) feels he has the opening, cuts to the basket, does not receive the ball and continues to the offside corner. The basic movement continues as (3) passes to (4), and goes to the baseline and out.

NOTE: One of the coaching points when teaching this offense is floor balance. The coach should constantly point out to the basic movers that when they have a mover in each of the four positions (in opposition to crowding one side of the court), the offense has the most chance to succeed. (Diagrams 1-9 and 1-10)

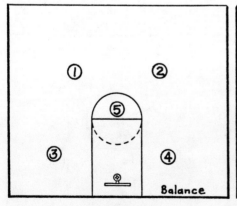

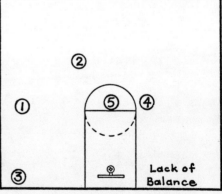

DIAGRAM 1-9   DIAGRAM 1-10

To maintain the type of balance desired, it is sometimes necessary for a player to dribble to a certain position, cut through and to the opposite corner (without handling the ball), or to double back and screen. We call these balancing moves.

The Pivot Man

One of the big decisions to make when using the four-man Passing Game plus a pivot man is where to play the pivot man. The four choices follow.

High Post. If the pivot man plays high at all times, he must be very strong at charging the boards and an excellent jump shooter. This method gives the four basic movers a lot of room to work and drive for the basket. (Diagram 1-11)

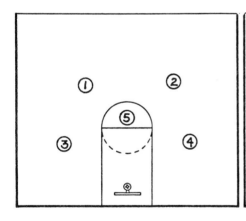 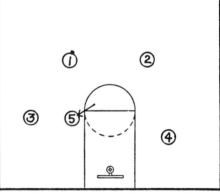

DIAGRAM 1-11   DIAGRAM 1-12

Onside Post. When one has a very strong pivot man, he may always swing him to the ball side. This will, in most instances, limit his teammates offensively to jump shots off the basic motion plus shots off the exchange when the ball is passed to the post. (Diagram 1-12)

Offside Post. One of the popular methods used in placing the pivot man is to station him in the low-post position opposite the

21

ball. This gives the basic movers plenty of room and keeps the pivot man (who is usually your top rebounder) in the most advantageous rebounding position. (Diagram 1-13)

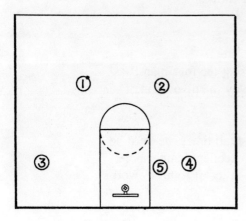

DIAGRAM 1-13

Roaming Post.   The roaming post position for the pivot man is a little more difficult to teach, but we advocate it because it adds so much to the offense. The pivot man (5) usually starts in a high-post position, although he may at times set up opposite the ball. He may cut to the ball side whenever a basic mover cuts between him and the ball. For example, in Diagram 1-14 guard (1) passes to forward (3) and screens opposite for guard (2). Guard (2) sees an opening, beats his man, and cuts for the basket off both (1) and the pivot man (5). Forward (3) could not pass to (2), so (2) cuts to a corner. In this situation it is the ball-side corner. Pivot man (5) is now free to swing to the ball-side post since (2) cut between him and the ball. (Diagram 1-14)

This now gives (3) the options of (a) continuing the basic movement by passing to either (4) or (2) and screening opposite for the other, or (b) hitting the pivot man (5) and splitting the post with (2). In this instance, the two offside men (4) and (1) would exchange. (Diagram 1-15)

Once the pivot man (5) has gone to a ball-side low-post position, he stays on that side until one of the basic movers has again cut

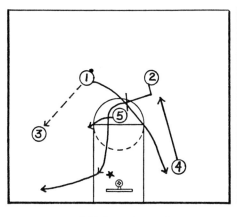

DIAGRAM 1-14

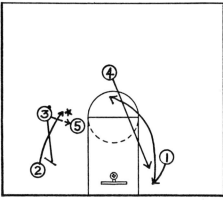

DIAGRAM 1-15

between him and the ball. Another common type of cut between the pivot man and the ball is a cut off him by the offside forward as shown in Diagram 1-16. The ball has been moved to the opposite corner by way of the basic Passing Game. Basic mover (3) takes the option of cutting off the pivot man.

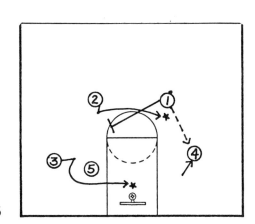

DIAGRAM 1-16

In Diagram 1-17, (3) was not open so he cleared to the ball-side corner. Since (3) cut between him and the ball, the pivot man (5) may now swing to the ball side. From here (4) may continue to run the basic movement or hit the post and exchange with (3).

23

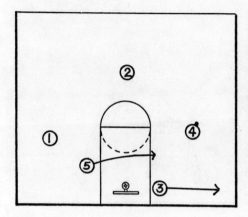

DIAGRAM 1-17

Again, in this event an offside exchange would be run by (2) and (1).

To repeat the pivot man's basic rule: *He may cut to the ball-side post any time anyone cuts between him and the ball. He may return to the high post at any time.*

The Passing Game offense, as with all offenses, is as strong as the players who run it. But, aside from simplicity, its strongest attribute is probably its unpredictability. It is very difficult to play against and even to scout, because the variables that compose it may be rearranged with every pass of the ball.

THE FOUR-MAN PASSING GAME AUXILIARY PLAYS

As the season wears on, plays may be added to supplement the offense. The following plays may be incorporated into the basic Passing Game without disrupting its continuity.

The Quick-Cut Play

At any time a passer may forego his offside screen and cut directly to the basket looking for a return pass. If he does not receive it, he goes to the far corner. (See Diagrams 1-18 and

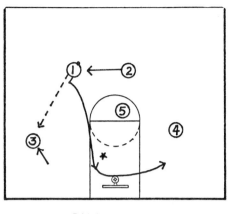

DIAGRAM 1-18

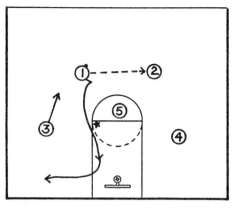

DIAGRAM 1-19

1-19.) In many cases, a cut of the sort shown will result in a give-and-go layup.

The Dribble-Chase Rule

Any time a dribbler brings his man toward you, clear and go to the nearest open corner. (See Diagrams 1-20 and 1-21.)

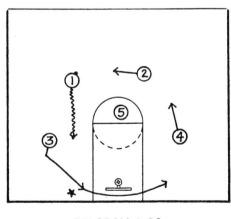

DIAGRAM 1-20

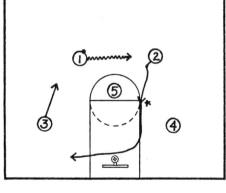

DIAGRAM 1-21

The other basic movers balance the offense.

This play gives the dribbler almost complete freedom to work on his defensive man. Also, the clear-out man can get a bounce pass for a layup if he changes direction and times his clear-out well.

The Second-Guard-Through Play

A play that fits very well in the rules of the Passing Game offense is the second-guard-through. This is accomplished, as shown in Diagram 1-22, when guard (1) passes to forward (3) and makes a quick cut to the opposite corner.

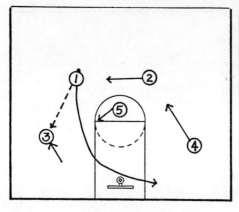
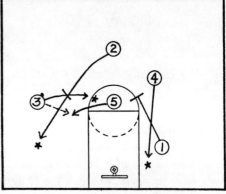

DIAGRAM 1-22   DIAGRAM 1-23

Forward (3) then passes to the post man (5) who has swung to that side and exchanges with (2) who becomes the second guard through. (Diagram 1-23)

Also to be noted in Diagram 1-23 is the offside exchange between (4) and (1). Since an inside man passed the ball to the post (5), both inside men cut first and are the screeners.

This is a play that is used by many teams. It meets all the requirements of the rules of the Passing Game.

The Backdoor Play

Once the pivot man (5) has swung to the ball-side low post, the offside corner man (4) in Diagram 1-24 may cut to the high post and receive a pass, which allows (2) to backdoor his man.

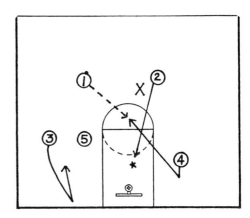

DIAGRAM 1-24

Player (1) then follows his basic rule of screening opposite for (3). (Diagram 1-25)

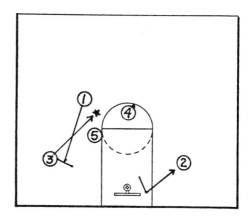

DIAGRAM 1-25

This move also works very well when the post man (5) is being fronted. Player (4) may lob to him for an easy layup shot. (See Diagrams 1-26 and 1-27.)

In the event (1) cannot pass to (4), he may run the basic movement by passing to either (2) or (3), or pass to (5) and split with

27

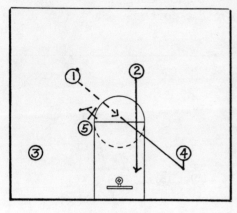

DIAGRAM 1-26

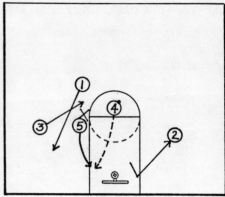

DIAGRAM 1-27

(3). Player (2) will not backdoor unless the pass goes inside to (4).

The Double-Inside Screen

When guard (1) in Diagram 1-28 passes to forward (3) and goes opposite to screen, the offside guard (2) may go with him and form a double screen for the offside forward (4). This can be run without disturbing the basic movement.

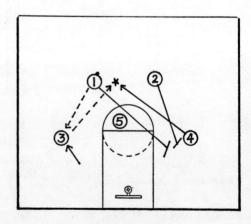

. DIAGRAM 1-28

NOTE: Since (2) was the first man to the corner, he will be the first out to balance the basic movement. Many times (4) can reverse the ball to (2) who has rubbed his man off on (1). (Diagram 1-29)

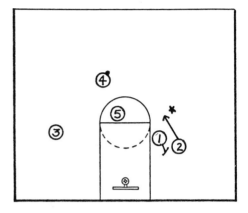

DIAGRAM 1-29

Another option of this play is for (2) to again come down for the double screen (for (4) who comes out high). Player (2) then runs his man into (1) and immediately cuts to the layup area. (Diagram 1-30)

This option works best against switching defenses.

DIAGRAM 1-30

The Stack

On a pass to the high post by a guard, both forwards may pinch in to form a stack on each side with the guards who have come down and inside the forwards. The guards then step out and the post man may pass to either the guards or forwards. (Diagrams 1-31 and 1-32)

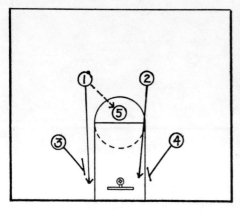

DIAGRAM 1-31

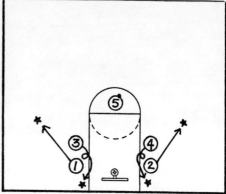

DIAGRAM 1-32

The Post-Opposite Play

In this play the post man (5) cuts to the offside post position on a pass from guard (2) to forward (4). On this key, forward (3) cuts off the screen and guard (1) loops around the post. (Diagram 1-33)

Guard (2) moves toward the opposite corner to screen. In this case, he forms a double screen with the post man (5) for (1) who loops around both of them to become the second option. (Diagram 1-34)

If neither (3) nor (1) is open, (3) clears to the ball-side deep corner. The post man then swings across the lane and the basic action is resumed.

30

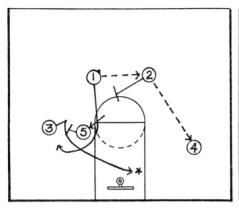

DIAGRAM 1-33

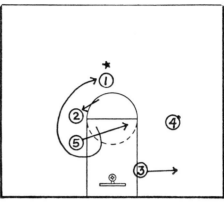

DIAGRAM 1-34

The Forward-Across Play

This play may be used in two ways:

(1) It is a good method of getting the ball to the forwards when they are being pressured and
(2) It works very well when the defense is switching.

In Diagram 1-35, guard (1) has passed the ball to guard (2) and gone to screen for his forward (3). In this case, the defense (X^1) and (X^3) have switched men.

DIAGRAM 1-35

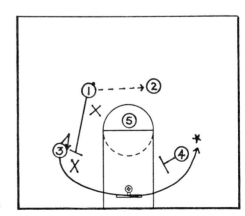

Instead of aiding the switch by coming out front, forward (3) goes opposite and around a screen set by forward (4) and takes a pass from (2) for a possible jump shot. (Diagram 1-35)

If player (3) cannot get the shot, (4) comes across to (3)'s original side and the basic Passing Game motion continues. (Diagram 1-36)

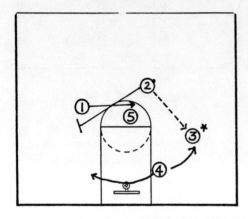

DIAGRAM 1-36

The Exchange-Switch Play

The same principle as described in the forward-across play may be used on an exchange play. In Diagram 1-37, guard (1) passed to the post (5) and came down to exchange with forward (3), but the defense switched. Seeing this, forward (3) would go across and around player (2) (who just exchanged with (4)) and receive a pass from the post man. (See Diagram 1-37.) Player (2) then swings around (1) on the opposite side for a possible jump shot. (Diagram 1-38)

The Over-the-Top Play

This play is keyed by breaking the basic pass-and-pick-opposite rule. When (1) passes to (3), (1) cuts outside. This keys the over-the-top play. Player (3) returns the ball to (1) and at the same time the offside forward (4) swings across the low-post area. (Diagram 1-39)

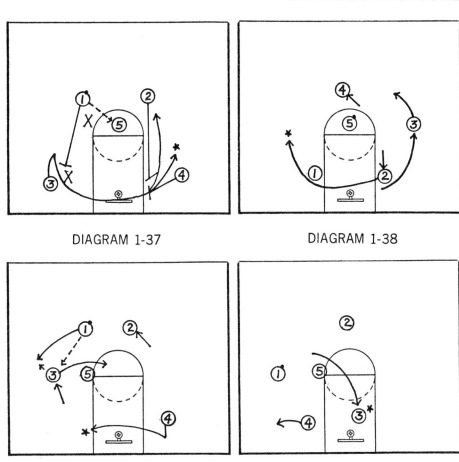

DIAGRAM 1-37

DIAGRAM 1-38

DIAGRAM 1-39

DIAGRAM 1-40

Player (3) then cuts over the post man looking for an over-the-top lob pass. Player (1) may pass to (4) in the low post, hit (3) with the lob, or continue with the basic pattern by passing to (2) or (4) (who has come to the corner) and screening opposite. (Diagram 1-40)

PASSING GAME SPECIAL CONTINUITIES

At times specific continuities that develop within the context of the Passing Game may be exploited. Some examples follow.

33

✳ A Reverse-Action-Type Continuity

Guard (1) passes to his forward (3) and screens opposite for the other guard (2). At the same time, (4), the offside forward, cuts off the post man (5) stationed in the offside low-post area. Forward (3) cannot pass to (4), so (4) continues to the ball-side corner. The post man then swings to the ball-side low-post area. (Diagram 1-41) Guard (1) continues to the offside corner.

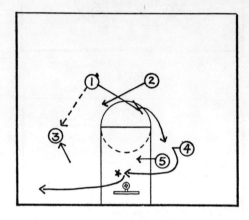

DIAGRAM 1-41

Player (3) then reverses the ball by way of (2) to (1). At the same time, both (3) and (2) follow their rule of screening opposite on each pass. (Diagram 1-42)

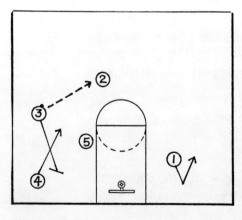

DIAGRAM 1-42

Once (1) receives the ball, the new offside corner man (3) cuts off the post (5) and the same sequence occurs on the opposite side of the court. (Diagrams 1-43 and 1-44)

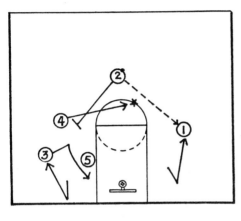
DIAGRAM 1-43

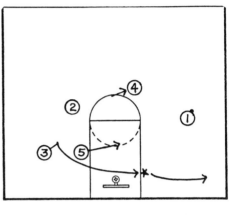
DIAGRAM 1-44

A Slashing-Type Continuity

Guard (1) passes to his forward (3). At the same time, the offside guard (2) slashes off the high-post man to the onside layup area. (See Diagram 1-45) Guard (1) continues to the offside corner and screens for (4), the offside forward.

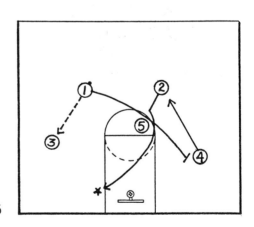
DIAGRAM 1-45

35

Player (4) comes off (1)'s screen to the head of the key. If (3) cannot hit (2), he passes to (4) and screens for the slasher (2). (Diagram 1-46)

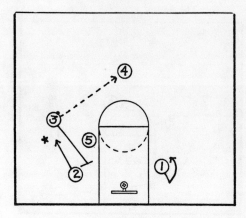

DIAGRAM 1-46

If (4) thinks (2) can get the easy jump shot, he passes to him. If not, (4) dribbles to his side to balance the offense and (2) continues his cut back out to his guard spot.

From here, the same sequence may be run again. (Diagram 1-47)

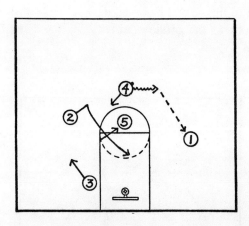

DIAGRAM 1-47

The play may now be run on either side, but, in this case, the ball is passed to (2) who passes to his forward. Player (4) screens opposite and this makes (1) the slash cutter.

A Double-Post-Stack Passing Game Continuity

This play, as the title denotes, has three basic movers and a double post. It begins when point man (1) passes to one of the wing men who have stepped out of the stack with the post man on their side. As shown in Diagram 1-48, (1) passes to (2).

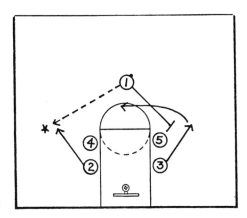

DIAGRAM 1-48

Point man (1) then screens opposite for the other mover (3). Player (2) can jump shoot, pass to the post, or pass to (3). In this case, (2) passes to (3) and both (2) and (1) go to the baseline, which, in effect, resets the stack. (Diagram 1-49) This is all done within the context of the Passing Game rules.

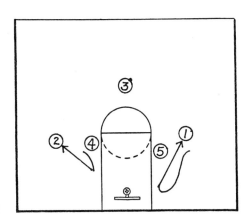

DIAGRAM 1-49

From here, new point man (3) may run the same option to either side.

The dribble-chase option works well with his continuity. Point man (1) may choose to dribble at either wing man, which will clear him. In Diagram 1-50, (1) dribbles at wing man (2) who clears. Point man (1) may now play two-on-two with the post man. (See Diagram 1-51.) Or (1) may reverse the ball to (2) by way of (3) who has come out front to balance the offense. (See Diagram 1-52.)

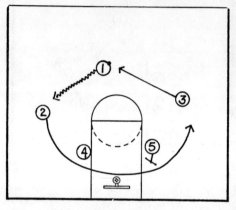

DIAGRAM 1-50

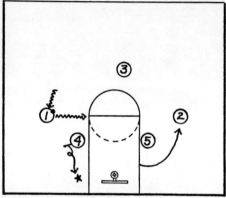

DIAGRAM 1-51

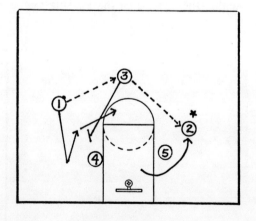

DIAGRAM 1-52

A Shuffle-Type Action

This play starts when guard (1) passes to his forward (3) and the offside guard (2) makes a slashing, shuffle-type cut off the post man (5) to the ball-side layup area. (See Diagram 1-53.) The guard who started the play comes down to screen the post man's defender. At the same time, the post man goes over and screens for the offside forward (4) who comes out front for a possible jump shot. (See Diagram 1-54.) Guard (1) by then catches up with the post man's defender and the post man becomes the third

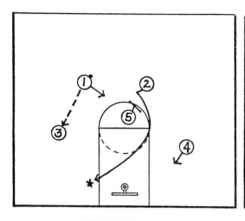

DIAGRAM 1-53

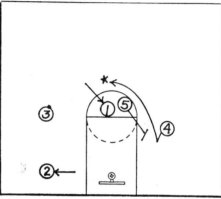

DIAGRAM 1-54

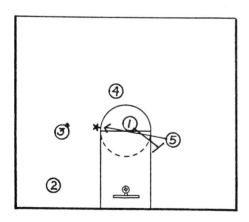

DIAGRAM 1-55

39

option by swinging back across the free-throw line to the ball side. (See Diagram 1-55.) If (3) feels none of the three cutters are open, he resets the play by dribbling out front and passing to (4). The new front man (4) then passes to his forward (1) and the shuffle action is run on the other side of the court. (Diagram 1-56)

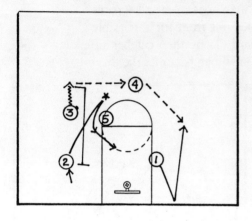

DIAGRAM 1-56

The Double-Cross Continuity

Guard (1) passes to his forward (3) and screens opposite for (2) who cuts to the ball-side layup area. Player (1) continues down and screens for forward (4) who comes out front for a possible scoring option. (Diagram 1-57)

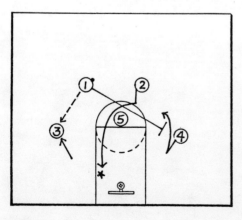

DIAGRAM 1-57

If (2) is not open, he continues across the foul lane area and screens for (1) who comes off the screen to the ball side. (Diagram 1-58)

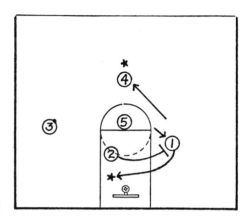

DIAGRAM 1-58

If none of the three options offers a good shot, (3) dribbles out front, passes to (4) who passes to his forward (2), and the continuity is run on the other side of the court. (Diagram 1-59)

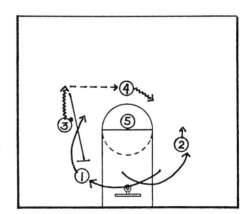

DIAGRAM 1-59

USING THE PASSING GAME AGAINST ZONE DEFENSES

One of the attributes of the Passing Game is adaptability. Following is a description of how it may be used against zone defenses.

The various offensive zone moves of cutting through, overloading and overshifting, rotating the zone players, screening the zone, splitting, and maintaining a passing and cutting tempo are shown in the context of the Passing Game.

Splitting the Defensive Perimeter

One of the primary moves against the zone defense is to prohibit it from matching your offensive perimeter. That is, against an odd front zone such as a 1-2-2 or 1-3-1 zone, you should have two men out front. (Diagram 1-60)

Against an even front zone such as a 2-3 or 2-1-2, you should have either one or three men out front. (Diagram 1-61)

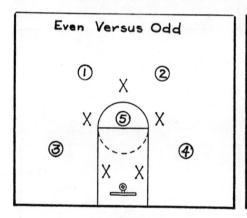

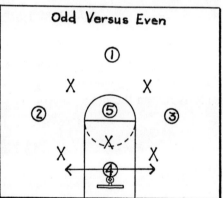

DIAGRAM 1-60   DIAGRAM 1-61

This even-against-odd and odd-against-even theory allows you to "split" the zone, that is, play your men between the zone defenders and confuse them as to their specific assignments. The Passing Game permits you to split any zone (even one that adjusts and tries to match your perimeter) by changing your perimeter with a very simple move.

Versus the Odd Front Zone. Since you start in a two-man front when running the Passing Game, this automatically splits an odd-man front zone. Although much movement takes place, the even-man offensive front is maintained because after each time one of the front men passes and cuts opposite to the baseline, another player comes out front. (Diagrams 1-62 and 1-63)

As you can see, in spite of the great amount of movement that takes place, the even-versus-odd advantage is maintained.

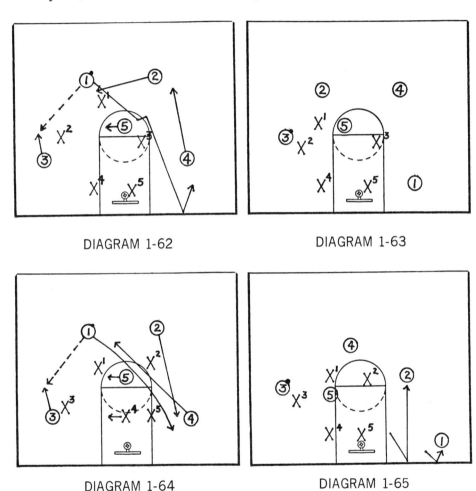

DIAGRAM 1-62   DIAGRAM 1-63

DIAGRAM 1-64   DIAGRAM 1-65

Versus the Even Front Zone. Against an even-man front, the Passing Game's usual even-man front may be converted to an odd front by having both guards cut through, as is often done against man-to-man defenses. (Diagrams 1-64 and 1-65)

As shown in these diagrams, both guards (1) and (2) cut through at the same time and (4) comes out. This converts you from an even to an odd front and splits the 2-3 or 2-1-2 zone. The trick to this play is for (2), the player who initiates the double cut through, to not come all the way back out after going to the baseline. He should come to a position between two of the zone defenders.

Cutting Through the Zone

The Quick Cut.   Another must maneuver against the zone defense is to cut through it. This is taken care of through the Passing Game play called the quick cut.

The sequence shown in Diagrams 1-66 through 1-69 is an example of what is probably the most common zone play operating completely within the rules of the Passing Game. In Diagram 1-66, front man (1) passes the ball to side man (3) and cuts through to the opposite corner. Players (2) and (4) fill the open areas nearest the ball and post man (5) swings to the ball side. Diagram 1-67 shows (3) passing the ball to (2) and going to the baseline. Post man (5) moves toward the high-post area. In Diagram 1-68, player (2) passes to (4) and screens opposite for (3). As shown in Diagram 1-69, sequence is completed when (4) passes the ball to (1) in the corner and starts a new one by making a quick cut to the opposite corner.

Another type of quick cut will result in an overload. Front man (1) passes the ball to the opposite guard (2) and makes a quick cut through the zone. (Diagram 1-70)

Player (3) takes the pass from (2) and may utilize the overload that has now been created. Player (2) then screens opposite for (4) as per rule.

Overloading and Overshifting

The Cross-Cut Play.   Another Passing Game play that is a functional zone move is shown in Diagram 1-71. Guard (1) passes to

44

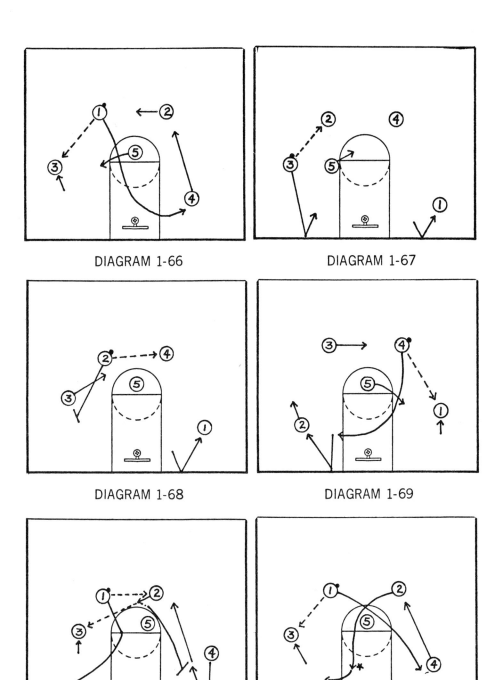

DIAGRAM 1-66

DIAGRAM 1-67

DIAGRAM 1-68

DIAGRAM 1-69

DIAGRAM 1-70

DIAGRAM 1-71

45

forward (3) and goes opposite. The other guard (2) cuts through the zone, looking for a pass from (3). These cuts by the two guards have done several things. They have:

(1) converted the offense to a one-man front, since (4) came out front.

(2) moved the post man to that side because (2) cut between him and the ball.

(3) created an overload, since (2) moved to the corner after his cut. (Diagram 1-72)

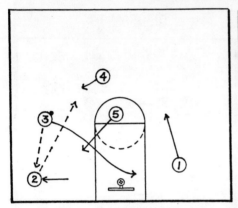

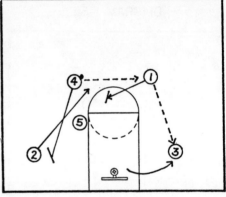

DIAGRAM 1-72   DIAGRAM 1-73

Player (3) then passes the ball to (2) in the corner and makes a quick cut through the zone. The ball is then reversed to him by way of (4) and (1) who make their cuts opposite after each pass. (Diagram 1-73) This converts us back to a two-man front and the sequence may be run again.

This play alone would be an adequate zone offense, when combined with a few quick cuts. It would be particularly difficult for an adjusting zone to defense.

Cutting Off the Low Post. One of the places most zones are vulnerable is in the middle at the high-post area. To take advantage of this, it works well to cut off the low post. The only adjustment that is made is to instruct the cutter to go to the high post instead of the ball-side low post.

As shown in Diagram 1-74, guard (2) passes the ball to the forward on his side, (4), and at the same time forward (3) cuts off the low-post man and goes to the high-post area. If he is not open, he swings to the ball-side post area. If he is still not open, he clears to the ball-side deep corner. (Diagram 1-75) The cutter has gone between the post man and the ball so the post man now swings to the ball side. This creates an overload. (Diagram 1-76)

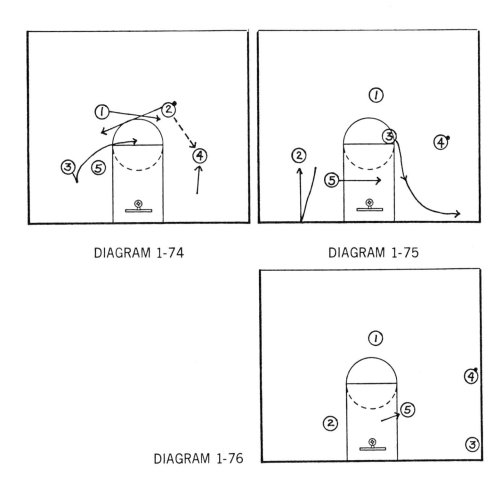

DIAGRAM 1-74   DIAGRAM 1-75

DIAGRAM 1-76

Rotating the Zone Players

The Dribble-Chase Against a Zone. The dribble-chase is a very fine move against a zone. It is very difficult to dribble

47

through a zone, but fairly easy to dribble around its perimeter. To repeat the dribble-chase rule: *If the dribbler comes toward you, clear and go to the nearest open corner.* In Diagram 1-77, guard (1) dribbles toward his forward who clears and goes to the opposite corner. In Diagram 1-78, the ball is returned to the front to (2). Player (2) then dribbles toward new front man (4) and this clears him to the opposite corner, which is open. Player (2) now has the option of passing to (3), who cut through from the opposite side, or, as shown in Diagram 1-79, reverse the ball by way of (1) to (4) who also had cut through from the opposite side.

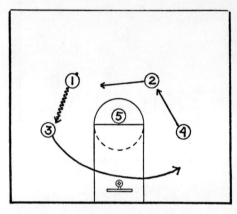

DIAGRAM 1-77   DIAGRAM 1-78

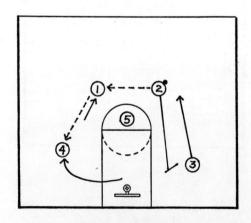

DIAGRAM 1-79

The dribble-chase works well against adjusting zones with man-to-man principles because the players are told to stay with the dribbler until he passes the ball. This pulls them out of their zone area.

Screening the Zone

The great amount of movement and screens away from the ball just naturally interfere with the zone's shifting and often results in easy jump shots. Some examples of this are shown in the following diagrams. (See Diagrams 1-80 through 1-83.)

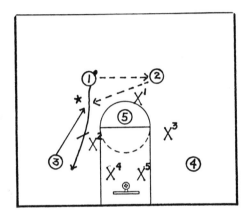

DIAGRAM 1-80
Guard-to-guard pass and screen offside wing

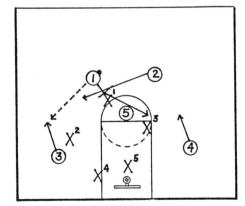

DIAGRAM 1-81
Guard-to-forward pass and screen of point man

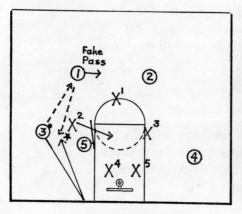

DIAGRAM 1-82
Forward-to-guard pass and
post screens sagging wing X^2

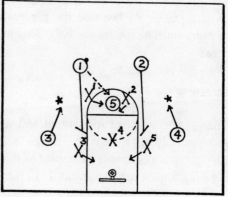

DIAGRAM 1-83
Pass to pass and screens by
guards to catch the zone sagging

Passing and Cutting Tempo

It is possible against a zone defense to cut *too* much. To prevent this when using the Passing Game as a zone offense, it is a good idea for no one to cut until and only if the passer cuts. If he does not cut, no one else moves. The next passer again has the option of moving or not.

TEACHING THE PASSING GAME OFFENSE

Personnel

One of the strengths of the Passing Game is that it allows a coach to use at least four players who are quite often very skilled, but are sometimes not tall enough to play forward and lack the mobility to be a true guard.

Coaching Points

Some of the attributes of the Passing Game that a coach should point out to his team and take advantage of are:

1. It utilizes the player of in-between height to full advantage.
2. It makes offside defensive help virtually impossible.
3. It allows opportunity for the players to play one-on-one and utilize their individual talents.
4. It is easy to restart the basic motion once it has been disrupted. This is not true with many continuity offenses.
5. It is a team attack. The number of shots is well divided between the players.
6. It makes better players because the guard and forward positions are interchangeable.
7. It provides both perimeter and penetration shots.
8. It complements a fast-break pressure-defense-type game.
9. It is adaptable to both switching and pressure-type defenses.
10. It helps your team's defense through playing against it in practice.

DRILLS TO TEACH THE PASSING GAME

Even though we play a four-man Passing Game, we feel it can best be taught by three-man situation drills.

Three-Man Shadow Drill

This very simple drill is necessary when introducing the Passing Game to your team.

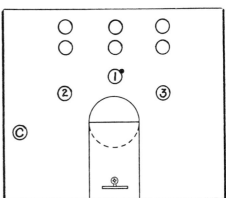

DIAGRAM 1-84

The team is placed in three lines at the head of the key as shown in Diagram 1-84.

Over.   The first man in each line steps forward with the middle man having the ball. The coach first calls out "Over." This tells them that we will first run the phase of the Passing Game where the middle man passes to either side and screens opposite. The cutter goes over the screen, receives a pass, and takes a jump shot. All three players rebound. (Diagram 1-85)

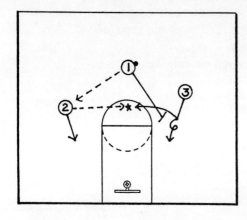

DIAGRAM 1-85

Some of the points to stress are:

1.   That the cutter (3) changes direction and comes off the screen by (1).
2.   That (1), after screening, rolls to the baseline.
3.   That (2) hit (3) with a crisp chest pass. After all three players go to rebound the shot, the next three men in line replace them.

✳   **NOTE: Another move that can be worked into this drill is to teach (3) to "bring his man up." He does this by faking a shot and causing his defender (who has just fought through a screen and is moving rapidly toward him) to get off-balance.**

Through.   Using the same player alignment, we next practice the cut through. When the middle man (1) passes and screens

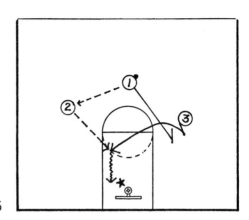

DIAGRAM 1-86

opposite, the cutter (3) takes the screen (after making a change of direction) and goes to the basket. (Diagram 1-86)

Upon receiving a pass from (2), he goes all the way to the basket and banks the layup.

Behind.   We use the same alignment, but add two dummy defenders to make the drill more realistic. (Diagram 1-87) When the middle man (1) passes and screens opposite, the man coming off the screen (3) fakes coming over the screen, but instead goes behind the dummy defender for a backdoor-type cut. In this situation we teach the passer (2) to hit the man cutting behind the dummy defender with a bounce pass.

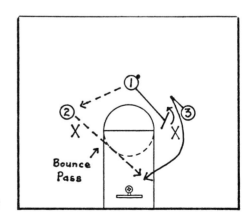

DIAGRAM 1-87

53

Back. We now remove the two dummy defenders, but put a player in each corner.

When we are working on the "back" move, the middle man again starts the play by passing and screening opposite. The man who was to utilize (1)'s screen joins him to form a double screen for the man in his corner (5). In effect, he has gone back. Player (5) comes off the double screen and can jump shoot or go to the basket. (Diagram 1-88)

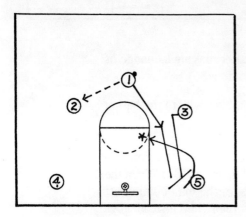

DIAGRAM 1-88

NOTE: We keep the same two men in the corner throughout this phase of the drill.

Shadow Drill from the Side Position

The players are then aligned as shown in Diagram 1-89 with the side man (1) starting the play.

From here we again work on the four basic moves:

1. Over
2. Through
3. Behind
4. Back

Each move is done repeatedly and on command from the coach.

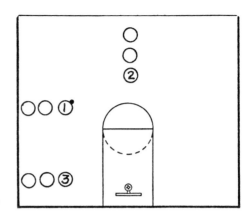

DIAGRAM 1-89

Shadow Drill from the Corner Position

When working out of the corner, we teach another important element of the Passing Game. When the corner man passes the ball to initiate the play, he must go to the baseline and back as shown in Diagram 1-90.

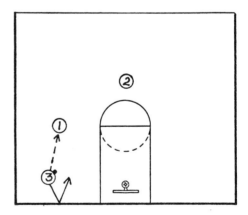

DIAGRAM 1-90

When working out of the corner, the players do not run the options on command. Once the middle man (1) has received the ball from the corner man (3) and the corner man (3) has gone to the baseline and back, the middle man (1) will pass to either side and screen opposite. The cutter may then choose to cut over, through, behind, or back.

55

Three-on-Three (Live)

We then play three-on-three half-court games with these rules:

A.   If you are the middle man and pass one way, you screen opposite.
B.   The cutter uses the screen with one of the options.
C.   If you are on the side and pass to the middle, you go opposite at least two steps toward the baseline.

In this way, we can practice what we have worked on in our shadow drills, but in a live situation.

We play games of seven baskets and the winners at one end of the court play the winners at the other end. The losers play the losers after they have run the stairs five times.

At least a week is spent on these three-man drills. Then the same drills are used, but from a four-man, two-guard, two-forward alignment. No pivot man is used until the pass-and-pick-opposite flow becomes second nature and the players can maintain floor balance. Once these things have been accomplished, we add the pivot man and teach the rules that involve him.

2

The Passing Game Shuffle

Probably the toughest offense we at Eastern Montana College have tried to defense is the Passing Game Shuffle, run by Dr. Jerry Krause's Eastern Washington teams, and Jack Ecklund at Rocky Mountain College.

THE PASSING GAME SHUFFLE VERSUS MAN-TO-MAN

This variation of the Passing Game starts in a 1-2-2 set and is built around the basic Passing Game rule to pass and pick opposite. As shown in Diagram 2-1, the ideal personnel for this offense are: a point man (1) who is a great dribbler who cannot be pressured; two big men (4) and (5); and two forwards (2) and (3) who have good size and adequate outside shooting ability.

The Pattern Set Move

Point man (1) starts the offense by dribbling his defender into either post man, (4) or (5), and working a basic screen-and-roll play. Point man (1) can take a jump shot or hit (4) as he rolls to the basket, as shown in Diagram 2-2.

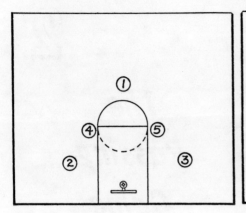

DIAGRAM 2-1

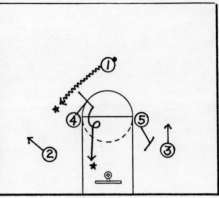

DIAGRAM 2-2

This move keys the other post man (5) to screen opposite for the offside forward (3), who uses the screen to move out to the head of the key. (Diagram 2-2) If (1) cannot get the jump shot or hit the roller, he may reverse the ball back to forward (3) who may be open for a jump shot.

NOTE: After offside post (5) screens opposite, he should roll to the basket in the event the defense has switched. (Diagram 2-3)

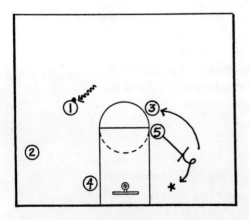

DIAGRAM 2-3

The Basic Shuffle

In that case, (1) may hit him with a cross-court lob or bounce pass. However, the basic play of this offense is the pass across the head of the key from (in the case of Diagram 2-4) guard (1) to forward (3). This keys the Shuffle action. As (1) passes to (3), (4) sets a blind screen on the defender of forward (2). Player (4) must step out actively and nail (2)'s man. Forward (2) uses this screen, cutting low off it, and across the lane. Player (3), who now has the ball, attempts to get the ball to (2), basket high. To make this play work, (5) must move out as if to get the ball from (3). (Diagram 2-4)

If 3 is denied pick back down on 5

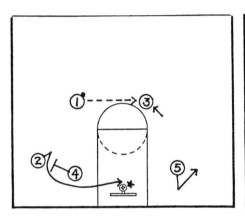 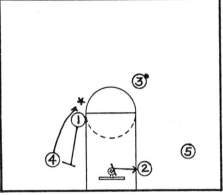

DIAGRAM 2-4   DIAGRAM 2-5

If forward (2) is not open by this cut, (1) follows his Passing Game rule of screening opposite after each pass. He screens for (4), who comes out front for a possible jump shot. This shot is open quite often because many times (4)'s defender will loosen up to help with (2)'s cut. (Diagram 2-5)

Thus a Shuffle action has taken place by the application of two rules:

(1) Pass and pick opposite.
(2) Each time the cross-court pass is made, the forward on the post side cuts off the post man.

59

Diagrams 2-6 and 2-7 show the Shuffle continuing by way of these two rules.

Player (3) throws the cross-court pass that keys the now strong-side forward (5) to cut off the player now in the post position (2).

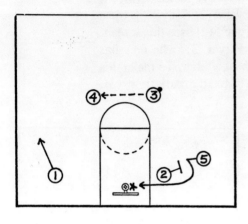

DIAGRAM 2-6

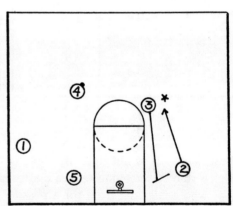

DIAGRAM 2-7

NOTE: Player (1) swings wide to clear the post area.

Player (3) then follows his Passing Game rule and screens opposite for (2).

NOTE: If (4) would return the ball to (2), the Shuffle would continue.

Diagrams 2-8 and 2-9 show the offense again from its beginning, but run in the opposite direction.

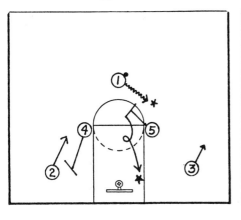 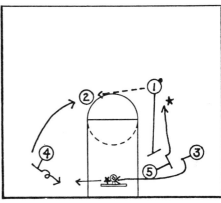

DIAGRAM 2-8   DIAGRAM 2-9

Other Methods of Starting the Passing Game Shuffle

Pass to the Forward and Cut Through.   To add variety to the offense, at times the point man (1) will pass to a forward and cut to the basket using the post man on that side to brush off his defender. (Diagram 2-10)

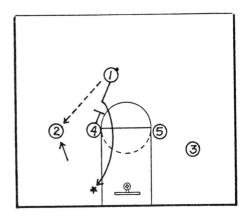

DIAGRAM 2-10

If (1) gets open, (2) may pass to him; if not, (2) works the screen and rolls with post man (4). (Diagram 2-11)

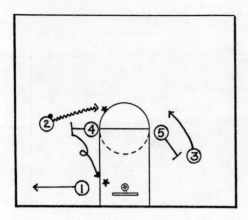

DIAGRAM 2-11

Point man (1) moves to the ball-side corner. At the same time, post man (5) screens for his forward who moves out front. The players are now in position to run the Passing Game Shuffle. (Diagram 2-12)

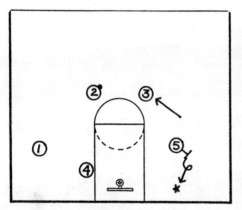

DIAGRAM 2-12   DIAGRAM 2-13

Pass and Screen Opposite.   Point man (1) passes to one forward (2) and screens opposite for the other forward (3). Forward (3) comes out front and the point man (1) rolls to the ball-side layup slot. (Diagram 2-13)

If (1) is not open, he clears to the corner and forward (2) works

the screen and roll with post man (4) (see Diagram 2-14) and the
players are then in position to run the Shuffle. (Diagram 2-15)

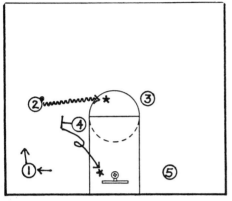 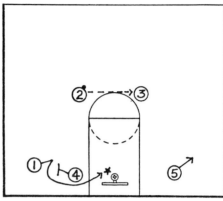

DIAGRAM 2-14   DIAGRAM 2-15

At times during this screen-opposite option, (3)'s defender will
fight over (5)'s screen and get ahead of (3). In this event, (3) has
the option of going backdoor to the ball-side post area. (Diagram
2-16)

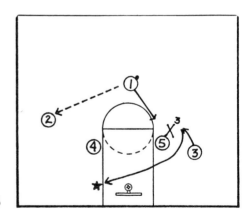

DIAGRAM 2-16

When this happens, (1) buttonhooks back and comes to the ball.
(Diagram 2-17) Players (2) and (4) work the screen and roll, (3)
clears to the corner, and the Shuffle is run. (See Diagrams 2-17
and 2-18.)

63

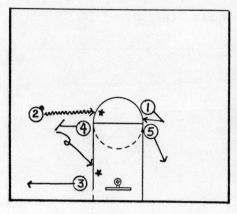

DIAGRAM 2-17

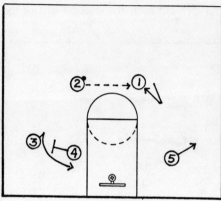

DIAGRAM 2-18

AUXILIARY PLAYS FOR THE PASSING GAME SHUFFLE

The Backdoor

When running the Passing Game Shuffle, the ball is always on the strong side of the court. That is the side of the court where three players are located. This fact remains constant for the simple reason that each time the ball is passed to the weakside, the strongside forward cuts off the post to overload the now ball-side. (Diagrams 2-19 and 2-20)

DIAGRAM 2-19

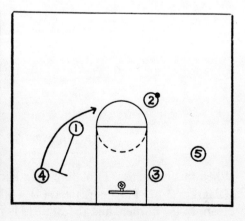

DIAGRAM 2-20

Because the ball is always on the strong side, the potential for a backdoor play always exists. The play is keyed when the now weakside forward (1) cuts to the high-post area as shown in Diagram 2-21 and receives a bounce pass from (2).

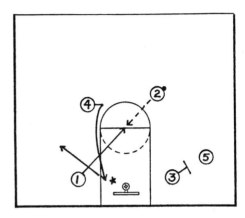

DIAGRAM 2-21

Player (4) goes behind his man and to the basket. If he does not receive a pass from (1), he wings out to the side.

Now post man (3) steps out and screens for (5) who hesitates until (4) has cleared to the side. Cutter (5) cuts low off the screen and looks for a pass from (1). Player (2) follows his Passing Game rule and goes down to screen for the first man opposite him, which in this case is (3). (Diagrams 2-22 and 2-23)

DIAGRAM 2-22

65

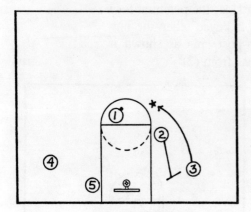

DIAGRAM 2-23

From here the players are back in the Passing Game Shuffle set and the play goes on.

The Second-Guard-Through Play

The players are in the Shuffle set and the ball is out front on the strong side in the possession of (1). In this case, (1) does not throw the ball cross the head of the key, but instead throws it to the strongside forward (4). (Diagram 2-24)

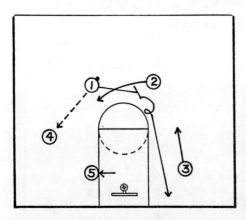

DIAGRAM 2-24

Player (1) again follows his Passing Game rule, which is: *When you pass the ball, screen opposite and go to the offside corner.*

66

Players (2) and (3) make their Passing Game rotations to fill the open spots. From here (4) hits the now post man (5) and goes opposite to screen. The next man in the rotation is (2). This is the second screen he has received and, in effect, he and (4) are splitting the post. (Diagram 2-25)

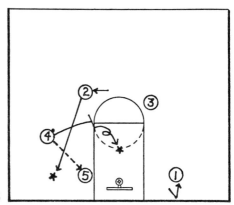

DIAGRAM 2-25

After (4) has screened for (2), he rolls down the middle looking for a pass from (5).

The Sagger Play

Many times as the Shuffle continues, the strongside forward's man will drop down behind the post man's screen before the cross-court pass that keys the cutters is made. (Diagram 2-26)

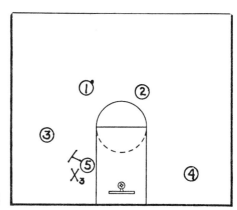

DIAGRAM 2-26

67

When this happens, post man (5) does not screen for (3) but instead when the pass from (1) to (2) is made, he slides back across the post. (Diagram 2-27)

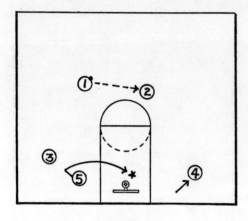

DIAGRAM 2-27

After his pass, (1) follows his Passing Game rule and goes to screen for the first man opposite him, which, in this case, is (3). Player (X^3) is really out of position and often (3) can get an unmolested jump shot. Also, if (5)'s defender has been hedging low to stop (3)'s cut, (5) may be open. (Diagram 2-28)

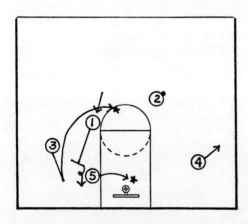

DIAGRAM 2-28

If neither of these options is open, the players are again in position to continue the Shuffle. (Diagram 2-29)

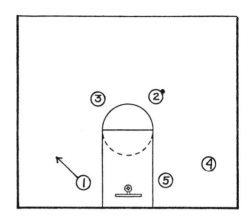

DIAGRAM 2-29

THE PASSING GAME SHUFFLE VERSUS THE ZONE DEFENSE

The initial move of the Passing Game Shuffle is a very unique one. In most of the basketball offenses used today, the teams start with a two-guard front and one guard cuts through, converting the perimeter to a one-man front. This maneuver has been utilized by a great many coaches. Against odd-man front zones, they simply tell their guards not to cut through and thus they initially split the zone. Against even-man front zones, they tell one guard to cut through and this results in a split of the even front zone.

Splitting the Zone

The Passing Game Shuffle starts with a one-man front and once the point man has dribbled off a post man, the offense converts to a two-guard front. This is a new picture for most zone teams because very few offenses operate in this manner. The Passing Game Shuffle team can utilize this fact in the following manner. If a team plays an even-man front against them, they can maintain their point offense and split the even front zone for easy shots. (Diagram 2-30)

If they face an odd front zone, all it takes is for the point man to dribble off one of the post men and the offense converts to an even front, which splits the odd front zone. (See Diagrams 2-31 and 2-32.)

69

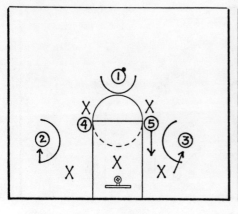

DIAGRAM 2-30

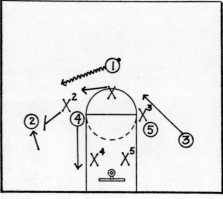

DIAGRAM 2-31

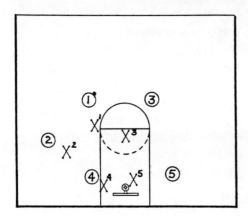

DIAGRAM 2-32

Utilizing the Overload Triangles

Once the guard has dribbled to either side, the offense has over-loaded one side. The triangles that make up this overload may be utilized by moving the ball. The ball should be passed to both sides of the court. The side of the court that is overloaded can be changed any time the ball goes to the weak side. All that has to happen is for the strongside forward to cut to that side of the court. (Diagram 2-33)

As seen in Diagram 2-33, it is more functional against zones for

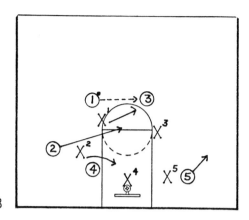

DIAGRAM 2-33

the cutter (strongside forward) to cut above the post and to the high-post area.

Screening the Zone

After the ball is reversed to the weak side, the men playing zone on the offside are usually assigned to sag off and help inside. The Passing Game Shuffle takes advantage of this by screening the saggers. In Diagram 2-34, the ball has been reversed to the then weak side and the strongside forward switches the overload by coming to that side and assuming the post position.

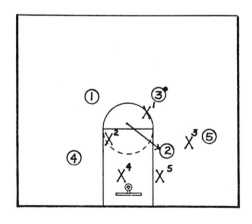

DIAGRAM 2-34

71

Offside defender (X^2) has sagged down to jam the high-post area. Player (1) comes down to screen for (4) as per assignment. In this case, he screens (X^2) and allows the ball to come back to (4) for an unmolested jump shot. (Diagram 2-35)

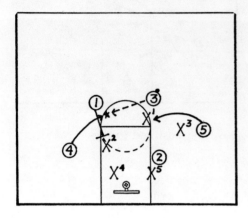

DIAGRAM 2-35

At the same time (5) cuts high and the Shuffle pattern continues. (Diagram 2-35)

Cutting Through the Zone

Another move that works against the zone defense is to use the point-guard-through method of starting the Passing Game Shuffle. That is the method where the guard (1) passes to a forward (2), cuts through to the baseline and on to the corner to create an overload. The forward (2) then has two options.

1. He may stay where he is and allow (3) to come to that side and maintain a one-man front offense (best against even front zones). (Diagram 2-36)
2. Or he may dribble out front and convert the offense to a two-man front (most functional against odd front zones). (Diagram 2-37)

This adaptability is a great tool for teams to have against adjusting zones.

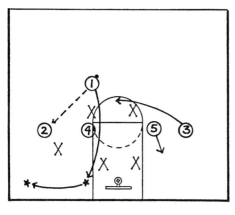

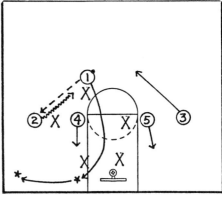

DIAGRAM 2-36   DIAGRAM 2-37

Thus it can be seen that the Passing Game Shuffle can be used as a zone offense. It allows a team to initially split, overload, over-shift, utilize triangles, switch the overload, screen the sagger, and cut through the zone defense. Its perimeter adaptability makes it functional against odd fronts (1-2-2, 1-3-1, and 3-2 zones), even fronts (2-3 and 2-1-2 zones), and adjusting zones.

TEACHING THE PASSING GAME SHUFFLE

Coaching Points

The Passing Game Shuffle actually has three phases:

1. The pattern set phase that allows a team to get into position to run the Shuffle and has scoring options of its own. (Three methods were mentioned including: screen and roll, pass to forward, and pass and pick opposite.)
2. The Shuffle phase, and
3. Other options that can and should be added as the season progresses.

Following are the coaching points that should be stressed when teaching this offense.

The Pattern Set Phase

Screen and Roll on the Point Guard.   When a post man sets a screen on the point man's defender, he must keep the rule covering this play in mind. If a blind screen is set behind the defender, he must give him room enough to turn and take a step. If the screen is from the side, he can really get close to the defender.

When the point man comes dribbling off the screen, he must look both for a jump shot and for the roller. The roller must never turn his back on the ball. The two most functional passes to use in this play are the bounce pass and the lob pass. The pass that causes the most problems is the line-drive pass that is easily intercepted or bounces off the finger tips of the roller. A well-thrown lob pass is one that were it not caught it would hit the floor inside the baseline. The two problems involved in the bounce pass are that it is often thrown too low or too hard. If it is positioned well, these things are not necessary. The man who sets the screen and rolls can help the passer by keeping his hands up, the nearest elbow to his defender high and his lead hand out as a target. (Diagram 2-38)

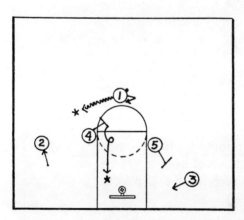

DIAGRAM 2-38

NOTE: It also helps the angle of the screen if the dribbler will fake in the opposite direction before coming off it.

The Offside Screen and Roll.   The screen away from the ball should be a Headhunter type. In Diagram 2-38 offside screener (5) has an angle on (3)'s man that allows him to screen him from the side and get as close as he desires. Also, since the screen is away from the play, the chance of a foul being made is minute. Player (3), the cutter, can help the screen by faking a cut toward the basket and waiting until the screener is set before moving toward the ball. After (5) sets the screen, he, too, should roll and look for a cross-court lob pass from (1).

The Shuffle Phase

The first concept to get across when teaching the Passing Game Shuffle is that it really is the Passing Game and that after each pass you screen opposite and go to the far baseline. Probably the best method of teaching this is to run the five-man Passing Game first and get the players in the habit of making this move.

Next, one must get across the idea that each time the guard-to-guard-type pass is made, the strongside forward must cut off the post and become the post man on the opposite side of the court. The main problem is to teach the man who has received the pass across the head of the key, (3), to hit the first cutter, (2), with the ball when he is basket high and not to wait too long. (Diagram 2-39) The coach must insist that when the strongside forward (2) cuts off the post, he must cut low, and when he feels he is open to go low down and spread out in order to disallow his defender to regain defensive position. (Diagram 2-39) The then weakside

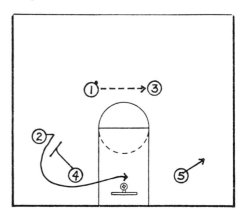

DIAGRAM 2-39

forward (5) must get this defensive man out of the post area by cutting to the side, free-throw line high, and keeping him busy. (Diagram 2-39) The post man who sets the screen for the strong-side forward must step out and set a definite screen. This not only helps the first cutter get open, but gives (1) a better angle to set his screen on the defender of (4). (Diagram 2-40)

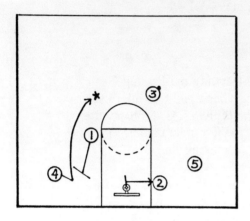

DIAGRAM 2-40

Other Options

The two options that must be added to make the offense work are, as previously mentioned, the backdoor and the second-guard-through.

The Backdoor Play. This play is a necessity for any team running any sort of continuity. It takes advantage of defensive overplay. When running the Passing Game Shuffle, the backdoor is keyed by the weakside forward who observes that the guard-to-guard pass cannot be thrown because the receiver is being pressured. He breaks up to the free-throw line and receives a bounce pass from the strongside guard. The bounce pass is best in this situation for two reasons: (1) it has the best chance of getting through, and (2) it allows the backdoor man to time his cut. When he spots his teammate cutting to the free-throw area, he becomes aware that the backdoor is developing and makes a step toward the ball. This pulls his defender up even more. When the bounce pass is made, the backdoor man starts his cut toward the basket as the ball hits the floor. Player (5) can then hit (3) with an under-scoop pass at the free-throw line or a bounce pass a split second later. If (3) doesn't get the ball, he wings out to the side and everyone else follows their rules. Player (1) screens opposite and (2) cuts off the screen by (4). (Diagram 2-41)

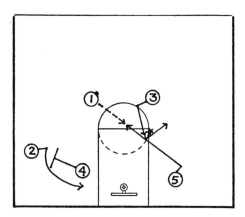

DIAGRAM 2-41

The Second-Guard-Through Play. This play involves split-ting the post. In Diagram 2-42, when (1) passes to (2) he follows his Passing Game rule of screening opposite. Player (2) then feeds the post man (4) and prepares to split the post with the next man in the rotation, (3). (Diagram 2-43)

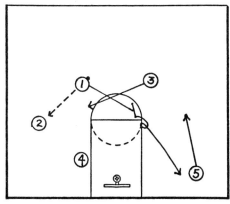

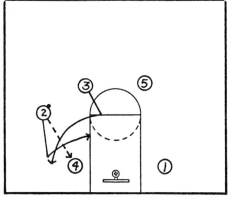

DIAGRAM 2-42   DIAGRAM 2-43

77

From here (2) and (3) must learn to read the defense. If they are not switching, (2) and (3) should change directions and brush very close. It is also a good move for (2) to set a definite screen on (3)'s defender and then roll to the basket. If they are switching, it is a good idea to fake the split and go backdoor on your man. This can be done by either (2) or (3). (See Diagrams 2-44 and 2-45.)

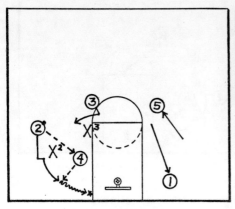

DIAGRAM 2-44
(2) backdoors the switch

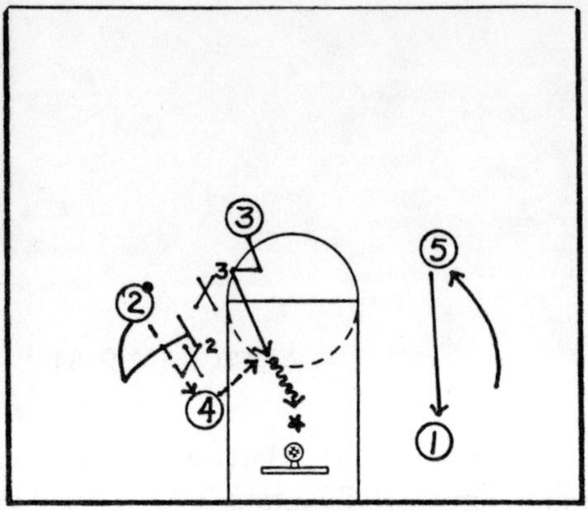

DIAGRAM 2-45
(3) backdoors the switch

In either case, (4) has room for a one-on-one play in the post because the other defenders in the play are kept busy.

DRILLS TO TEACH THE PASSING GAME SHUFFLE

The Screen-and-Roll Drill

The first drill to be worked on is the simple screen-and-roll involving the point man and the post man. (Diagram 2-46)

This drill is run live, and (4) and (1) attempt to score on the screen-and-roll play. The same two men play defense until they have stopped three consecutive plays. Two new offensive players are involved each play.

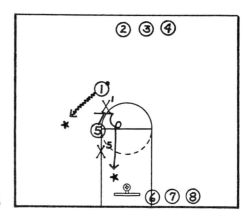

DIAGRAM 2-46

The Offside Screen-and-Roll Drill

Four offensive players are involved in this drill. Players (1) and (4) work the simple screen-and-roll with no defenders. Players (5) and (3) work the offside screen-and-roll with defenders on them. The play must be made to the offside; that is, (1) cannot shoot or pass to (4), but must hit (3) for a jump shot or (5) with a cross-court lob. (Diagram 2-47)

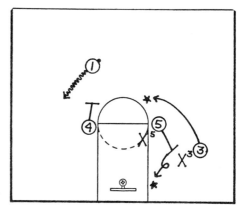

DIAGRAM 2-47

The defense is told to react in a particular way (switch or fight over) according to what the coaches are working on. Again, the two defenders must stop three in a row. The same two players

79

make the simple screen-and-roll until the coach changes people. Two different offensive players are involved in the offside screen-and-roll in each new play.

The California Drill

As shown in Diagram 2-48, the coach starts the drill by passing the ball to (3) on the weak side of the court. Player (2) then screens opposite for (1) who changes direction and cuts low to the ball. Player (3) passes to (2) if he is open. If not, (3) reverses the ball to (2) by way of the coach. Player (3) then cuts off screener (1), looking for a pass from (2). (Diagram 2-49) If (2) cannot get the ball to (3), it is again reversed to the weak side. This time (1) becomes the feeder. This process continues until the offense scores or the defense secures the ball. (Diagram 2-50)

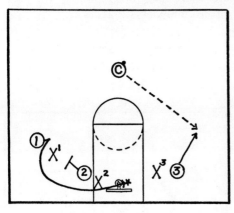

DIAGRAM 2-48

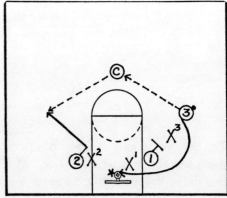

DIAGRAM 2-49

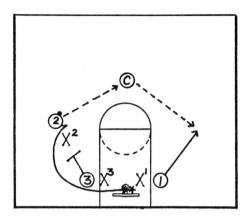

DIAGRAM 2-50

Again, the three defenders must stop the offense three times straight. Each time a basket is made or the defense secures the ball, three new offensive players come in.

The Strongside Recognition Drill

Two teams compete against each other on a half-court basis in this drill. The ball is given to the strongside guard and he can call one of three plays:

1. If he passes cross-court to the other guard, the two Shuffle phases are run. (Diagram 2-51)

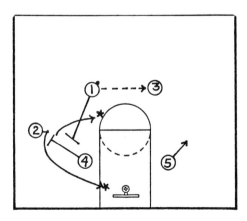

DIAGRAM 2-51

81

2. If he passes to the strongside forward, the second-guard-through play is run. (Diagram 2-52)

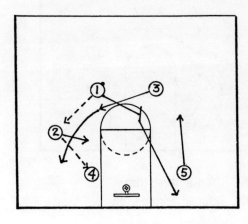

DIAGRAM 2-52

3. If he hits the weakside forward cutting to the high post, the backdoor play is run. (Diagram 2-53)

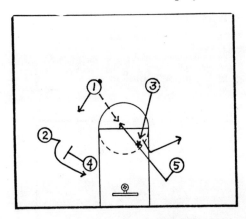

DIAGRAM 2-53

The play is run until they score or lose the ball. A team is given five such opportunities and then the other team gets five chances. The team that scores the most out of five is the winner and the other runs three wind sprints.

NOTE: To warm up mentally and physically, this recognition drill is run first with no defense.

Progressive Sequence of Offensive Drills

1. Half-court offense; repeat the parts over and over (no defense).
2. Half-court offense run as a continuity three times around and then a shot (no defense).
3. Half-court scrimmage (five-on-five).
4. Full-court scrimmage; no fast break.
5. Full-court controlled scrimmage. If a team scores, they get the ball back.
6. Full go. Take the fast break and if it isn't there, run the offense.

3

A
Post-Oriented
Stack
Offense

One of the weaknesses of a one-man front offense is that you must have a point guard who can dominate the action. He must be able to operate in spite of defensive pressure. This guard is not easy to find. The strength of the one-man front offense is that it allows a coach to play two big post men at the same time and keep both of them in the pivot play area.

THE POST-ORIENTED STACK VERSUS MAN-TO-MAN

The following offense utilizes two big men in the post area, but is run from a two-guard situation. The basic personnel alignment is: two guards out front (1) and (2), an average-sized forward on the weak side (3), and a stack on the strong side featuring the big post man (5) on top and the big forward (4) low. (Diagram 3-1)

NOTE: Strong side again refers to the side of the court with the greatest number of offensive players.

Weakside Action

When the weakside guard (1) passes to the forward (3) on his side, the post man (5) cuts low to that side and the big forward (4) cuts to the high-post area. (Diagram 3-2)

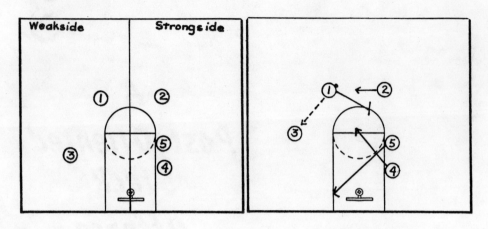

DIAGRAM 3-1   DIAGRAM 3-2

Either of them may get open during this crossing action. At the same time the guards cross with the guard (1) who initiated the play, making a definite screen on the defender (2) of the other. From here, either of two plays may be run.

Split the Low Post.   Forward (3) may pass to the big post man (5) and split the post with the guard (2) coming his way. (Diagram 3-3)

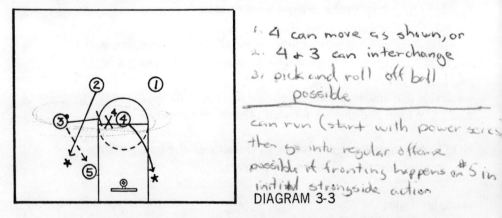

1. 4 can move as shown, or
2. 4 & 3 can interchange
3. pick and roll off ball possible

can run (start with power series then go into regular offense possible if fronting happens on #5 in initial strongside action

DIAGRAM 3-3

Big forward (4) cuts to the basket in the far layup lane and at times his man may be caught looking at the play, which results in a quick pass to (4) for an easy basket. This happens more often

one on one keep score (shooting low)

pick & roll strong side

than one would think because (4)'s defender often attempts to get between (4) and the ball.

The Backdoor.   Again, weakside guard (1) passes to the forward on his side and crosses with the other guard. This time forward (3) chooses to pass to the big forward (4) cutting to the high-post area. (Diagram 3-4)

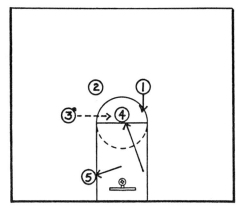

DIAGRAM 3-4

The big forward (4) looks first for a jump shot and second for guard (1) who has backdoored his defender. If (1) is not open, he continues down and forms a moving screen for the big post man (5) moving across the low-post area. (Diagram 3-5)

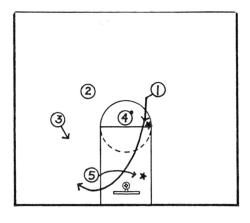

DIAGRAM 3-5

87

If neither (1) nor the big post man (5) is open, (3) pinches in for (1) and (1) can be open for a jump shot or, if a switch is made, (3) may be open in the low-post area. (Diagram 3-6)

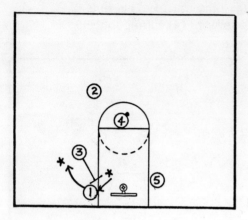

1. if pass is made to 1, look for shot, 2. look to 3 posted up.
3. If pass not made to 3, 3 picks across lane for 5.

If no pass to 1, 4 can shot after 3 picks across (then reverses pivots for position) and 5 breaks across

DIAGRAM 3-6

Two other plays happen quite frequently because of the nature of today's defenses. When the big post man (5) breaks to the ball, his defender will often play him three-quarters to the ball or even front him. In this case, one of two things may happen:

1. Player (3) may lob the ball to (5). This can happen because (4) has taken the weakside help away by cutting the high post. (Diagram 3-7)

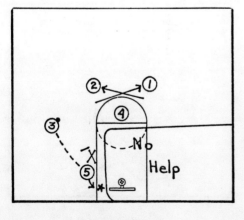

1. if pass to 5, 4 goes to backside rebounding position quick
2. unless 5 is fronted, after 4 passes to 3, 4 moves to backside rebounding position

DIAGRAM 3-7

2. When (4) receives the pass in the high-post area, (5)'s defender may be caught out of position and (5) may be able to pivot inside for a lob pass from (4). (Diagram 3-8)

4. 4's pivot might be
reverse pivot. Possibly
a better angle for #5.
#5 position important
drill on 3 on 3 action (
feeding post

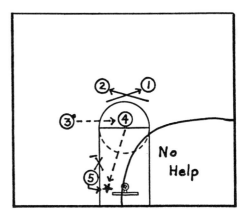

DIAGRAM 3-8

Strongside Action

When the play is initiated on the strong side, the offense gains the advantage of working out of a basic Stack play. (This play is best described in Ed Jucker's book *Power Basketball*.) In essence, what happens is that the forward (4) steps out of the Stack and attempts to rub his man off on the post (5). If no switch is made, the forward should be open for a ten- to twelve-foot jump shot. (Diagram 3-9)

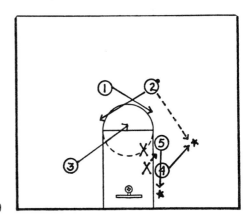

DIAGRAM 3-9

If a switch is made, you have a big-little mismatch in the pivot area with the big offensive post man (5) at a great advantage. (Diagrams 3-10 and 3-11)

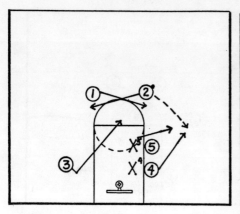

DIAGRAM 3-10

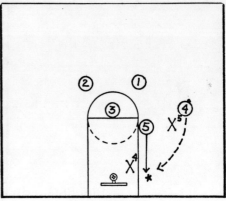

DIAGRAM 3-11

After the pass is made to the forward (4), the offside forward (3) breaks to the high-post area to take away the offside help. From here, the same options are run as for weakside action.

POST-ORIENTED STACK OFFENSE AUXILIARY PLAYS

The following plays should be added to the Post-Oriented Stack Offense.

The Wall Play

When running weakside action, the wall play can be run and still lead to the same two basic options (split and backdoor). This play starts when the weakside guard (1) passes to the forward on his side (3) and, instead of crossing with the other guard, goes down and around the Stack on the other side. (Diagram 3-12)

The post man (5) and the big forward (4) make their same basic moves. Player (3) may now work the two basic options or reverse

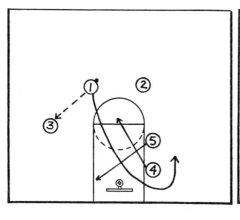

DIAGRAM 3-12

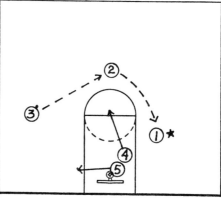

DIAGRAM 3-13

the ball by way of guard (2) to (1) who has lost his man on (5) or (4). (Diagram 3-13)

The Wall Play Outside Cut

This same play may be run from an outside cut key. Weakside guard (1) throws the ball to the forward on his side and makes an outside cut. Player (3) gives the ball back to (1) and goes down and around the wall on the other side of the court. From here the same options prevail with (1) and (3) changing assignments. (Diagrams 3-14, 3-15, and 3-16)

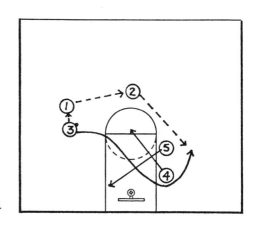

DIAGRAM 3-14

91

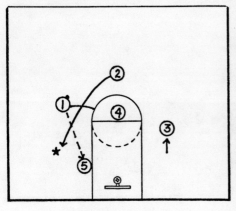

DIAGRAM 3-15

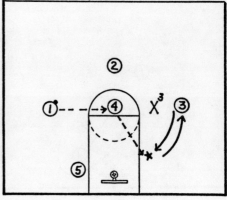

DIAGRAM 3-16

✳ The Backdoor Play

From the strong side, a backdoor play may be run. Weakside forward (3) keys the play by cutting to the high-post area. Strongside guard (2) hits him with a bounce pass. Player (1) backdoors his man (his man was expecting him to cross with (2) and was overplaying him that way). (Diagram 3-17) *also...*

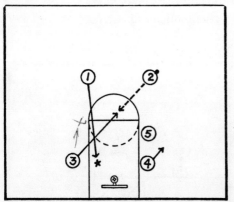

5 can pick down, 4 breaks out then (a.) 3 can hit 4 for a short jump shot or feed (5). (b.) break back past 5 for pass from 3. If 4 not open

X pick and roll key – weakside man breaks to high post spot when weakside guard has ball.

DIAGRAM 3-17

If (1) does not get the ball from (3), he continues down and around the post man (5) who attempts to rub his man off on him as he slides across the low-post area. (Diagram 3-18)

92

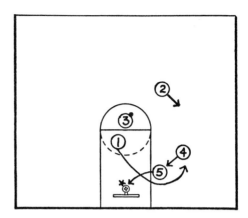

DIAGRAM 3-18

If this isn't open, (1) continues around (4), and (3) may look for (1)'s jump shot or (4) inside. Player (2) changes direction and comes back for a possible jump shot. (Diagram 3-19)

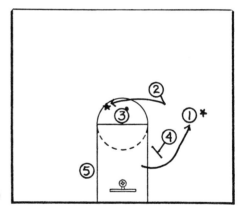

DIAGRAM 3-19

THE POST-ORIENTED STACK OFFENSE VERSUS THE ZONE DEFENSE

This offense may be run against a zone with the same patterns but with the priorities changed.

Weakside Action

When the ball is at the weakside guard (1) position, he again gets the ball in to his forward (3) and crosses with the other guard (2).

When (1) goes across, he loops down to a position almost as deep as the free-throw line extended for a potential cross-court pass. The post man (5) and the big forward (4) make their normal crossing moves. (Diagram 3-20)

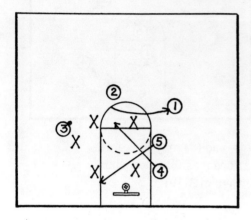

DIAGRAM 3-20

Pass to High Post. If forward (3) passes to the high post, (4) looks first for the player who would be the backdoor man against man-to-man defenses (player (1)). Player (1)'s instructions are that when the ball goes to the high post, he should find a hole on the weak side for a short jump shot. The man at the high post (4) should also look inside to the big post man (5). (Diagram 3-21)

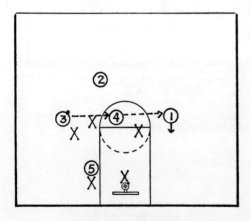

DIAGRAM 3-21

94

A very good play for (4) to make is to fake it to (1) and then put up a lob pass to the big man (5) inside. (Diagram 3-22)

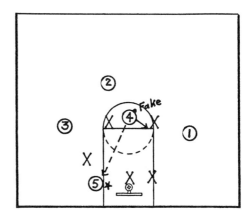

DIAGRAM 3-22

All this time (2) acts as a safety valve for (4). If (1) is covered, he keeps coming around the post man (5) to the far corner. This overloads that side. (Diagram 3-23)

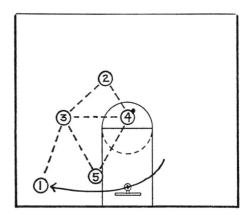

DIAGRAM 3-23

Player (3) and the post man (5) do not move as per their man-to-man assignments. The ball is then moved until a good shot arises.

Pass to Low Post. When the weakside guard passes to the forward on his side he again crosses with the guard. The post man

(5) breaks low out of the Stack as usual and the big forward (4) goes high. This time the forward (3) passes to the big man (5) in the low post. If he is one-on-one, he shoots it. At the same time the high-post man (4) breaks down looking for a play that U.C.L.A. made famous with Walton and Wilkes. Many times (4) will be open. (Diagram 3-24) If not, (3) and (2) split the post. (Diagram 3-25) Player (3) tries to pull the zone in so (2) can get a jump shot.

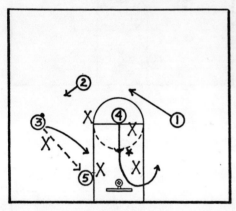

DIAGRAM 3-24

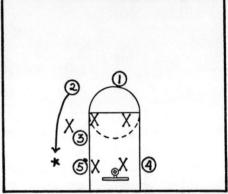

DIAGRAM 3-25

Player (1) moves back for defensive balance and (3) continues to the offside wing position. The ball is then moved until a good shot is forthcoming.

The Wall Play. One of the facets of this offense that works extremely well against zones is the wall play. Weakside guard (1) passes to his forward (3) and the zone shifts in that direction. Guard (1) goes down and around the wall, which, in this case, stays together and the ball is quickly reversed to (1). The post man (5) and (4) prevent the zone from getting back to cover (1). (Diagrams 3-26 and 3-27)

This same thing, of course, may be run from an outside cut with (3) and (1) changing assignments.

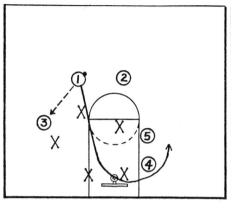

DIAGRAM 3-26

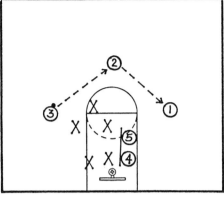

DIAGRAM 3-27

Strongside Action

The Stack play may be run against zones if one extra pass is made. The strongside guard must throw the ball to the weakside guard who fakes to his forward, then lobs the ball back to (4) stepping out of the Stack. (Diagrams 3-28 and 3-29)

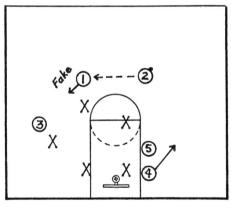

DIAGRAM 3-28

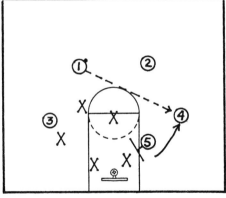

DIAGRAM 3-29

From here, the guards cross, (3) cuts to the high post, and the same options prevail. (Diagram 3-30)

97

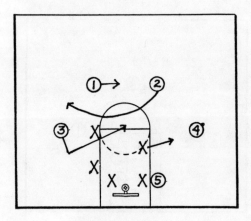

DIAGRAM 3-30

TEACHING THE POST-ORIENTED STACK OFFENSE

Coaching Points
Weakside Plays

The Crossing Action. When the ball goes to the weakside forward (3), the post (5) and the big forward (4) must make the cross move to get to their respective high and low post positions. A lot of things can happen from this maneuver. If the forward's (4) defender is playing loose to give potential help to the defender of (3), the post man (5) should screen him. This may result in an uncontested shot for (4) from the free-throw line. (Diagram 3-31)

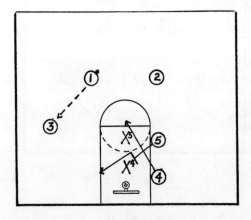

DIAGRAM 3-31

Another possibility if (X⁵) and (X⁴) are playing loose is for (4) to screen the post man's defender and for (3) to lob cross-court to the post man (5). (Diagram 3-32)

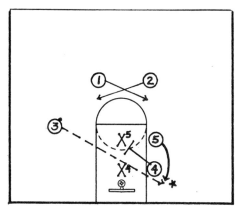

DIAGRAM 3-32

If the defenders on (4) and the post (5) are playing tight and not switching, the post man (5) should just take a step forward and stop and (4) should go off him trying to rub off his man.

If the defense is switching, the post man (5) and forward (4) may fake crossing and the post man (5) cuts to the high post as the forward goes to the low-post position. In effect, they have changed jobs and the defense may get mixed up by the new picture. (Diagram 3-33)

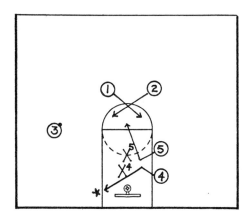

DIAGRAM 3-33

The David Thompson Play. An option that may be added if you are fortunate enough to have a great leaping forward is a cross-court lob pass to the offside forward.

When the weakside guard (1) passes to his forward (3), it keys the post (5) and big forward (4) to cut to their low-post and high-post positions. After the forward has cut to the high post a few times, his defender will try to do what his coach taught him and that is to beat (4) to the spot and not trail him across the lane. When this happens and (4) is having trouble getting the ball, he should come out toward the high post slowly for the first few steps to allow his defender to get ahead of him, then take a couple of quick steps causing his opponent to get all of his weight forward, then (4) should push off his front foot and backdoor for a cross-court lob. (Diagrams 3-34 and 3-35)

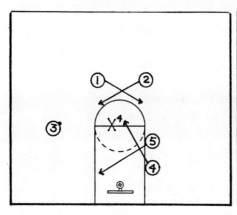 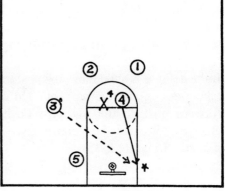

DIAGRAM 3-34   DIAGRAM 3-35

This offense is especially well suited for this play because the crossing movement of the guard takes away any defensive help (X⁴) might have. It may be run from either the weak or strong side.

NOTE: Once (4) has made his backdoor move and is ahead of his man, he must maintain that position by spreading out and keeping the elbow closest to the defender up. Timing this cut and pass requires a lot of practice time.

100

The Backdoor Play. When the ball is passed to the forward (4) in the high-post area, the backdooring guard (1) changes direction and goes to the basket. At this point, the post man's defender (X⁵) will probably loosen up to help. If the forward (4) in the high post is alert, he may be able to fake the backdoor man and hit the post man (5) for a power layup play. (Diagram 3-36)

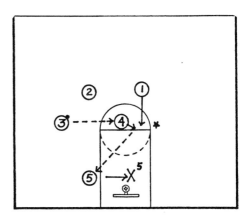

DIAGRAM 3-36

Of course, if the backdoor man is open, he is the first option. After the backdoor part of the play is over, the guard (1) must cut close to the post man (5) and the post man (5) must use him. When the post man (5) receives this pass, he must be able to read his defender and pivot away from him for a jump shot or hook shot. (Diagrams 3-37 and 3-38)

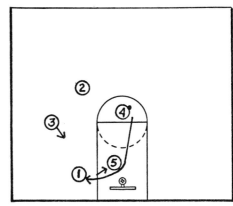

DIAGRAM 3-37

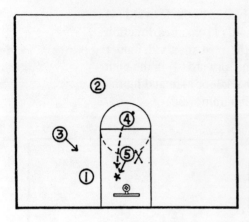

DIAGRAM 3-38

If (5) is not open, he clears the lane and (3) pinches for (1) who can help this play work if he will stop and get his defender on his back. This also prevents a blocking foul on (3) who would run into (1)'s defender if he were on the move. (Diagram 3-39)

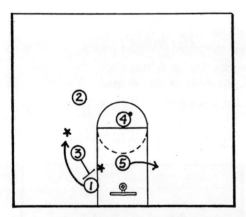

DIAGRAM 3-39

NOTE: If, at any time, (4) is pressured, (2) is the safety valve man.

The Low-Post Split Play. When the ball goes to the post man (5) in the low-post area, (3) splits the post with the guard coming his way. The point to emphasize is that the post man (5) must be told that this is his one-on-one play. The first option is for him to shoot. If he cannot, he looks for (4) backdooring out of the high post or (3) and (2) splitting the post.

Strongside Action

When the play is initiated from the strong side, it starts from the Stack play, which is so ably described in Ed Jucker's book *Power Basketball*. After the Stack phase is over, the same options prevail as they do in weakside action.

DRILLS TO TEACH THE POST-ORIENTED STACK

The Stack Drill

Much time is spent on the strongside guard feeding the forward coming off the Stack. The options stressed are that the forward may: jump shoot, feed the post man (5) away from his defender, drive the baseline and look for the post man (5) rolling if the post man's defender picks him up, lob to the post man, or backdoor and clear if the pass from the strongside guard goes to the post man.

The Cross Drill

The cross drill is worked on against various defenses. For example, a defender is placed on (4) and told not to let him get the ball in the high-post area. The feeder (3) is told that if (4) is open to get the ball to him, not to hit the low-post man. The cross is made and (4) attempts to open on the cross. If the defender is tough, (4) may try the David Thompson play or backdoor out of the high post when the ball goes to the low post. Forward (4) soon learns that his options make it very difficult for the defender to pressure him.

The Basic Plays Drill

Time is then spent on the two basic maneuvers of this offense —the split and the backdoor.

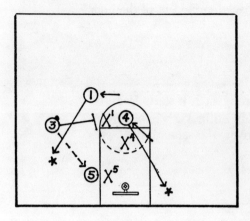

DIAGRAM 3-40

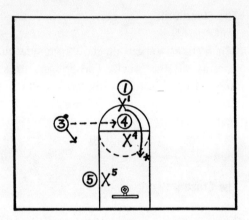

DIAGRAM 3-41

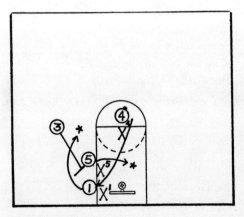

DIAGRAM 3-42

Option keys

Strongside / Weakside

1. Split low post — pass to
   wing ⟹ <u>pass to low post</u>

2. Backdoor — <u>pass to high post</u>
   from guard or wing

* note: if high post passes
   to wing ⟹ then to low post-
   split can still be run.
   Backside guard merely assumes
   combination backside rebounding/
   safety position

3. Pick and Roll — weakside
   post breaks to high post spot
   if weakside guard has ball

The Split. Three offensive men and three defensive men are used on this drill. The ball is given to the man in the forward position. He attempts to pass to the low post and split with the guard. They must read the defense and the forward may lob to the post if he is overplayed, pass to the post and make a definite screen for the guard, or fake the split in the event of defensive switch. The defense must stop the offense three times straight. A new trio of offensive players come in on each new play.

The Backdoor. This drill involves four offensive players. Only one guard is used. There are three defensive players: one on the guard, one on the post man, and one on the Stacking forward. The ball is given to the weakside forward (3). He bounces the ball to start the drill. The post (5) and the big forward (4) cross and come toward the ball. If the ball goes to the low-post area, the big forward (4) breaking to the high-post area backdoors and the one guard (1) splits the post with the weakside forward (3). (Diagram 3-40)

If the ball goes to the big forward (4), the guard (1) backdoors and if he isn't open, the post man (5) cuts off him. (Diagrams 3-41 and 3-42) Any time (5) or (4) get open on the cross, they may shoot. Three new offensive players come in after each play. The defenders must stop three plays in a row.

4

The High-Post Wall Offense

THE HIGH-POST WALL VERSUS MAN-TO-MAN

The primary man-to-man offense used at Eastern Montana College consists of three plays. We call it the High-Post Wall. It is an ideal offense for a team that lacks the strong pivot man. Placing the post man high opens up the lane and offers room for the forwards to play one-on-one and for the guards to cut through and post their men when they have a size advantage.

The Inside Cut

This play starts when guard (1) passes the ball to the forward (3) on his side of the court, and goes to screen for the offside guard (2). He along with the high-post man (5) form a wall. Guard (2) steps toward guard (1), changes direction, and slashes off the high-post man (5) to the ball-side layup slot. If (2) is open, (3) passes to him for an easy layup. (Diagram 4-1)

If (2) is not open, (3) may pass:

1. To the post man (5) who has moved toward the ball. In this event (3) then goes in and screens for (2) who comes out for a short jump shot. (Diagram 4-2) The post man (5) also has the options of jump shooting if his man has loosened up to

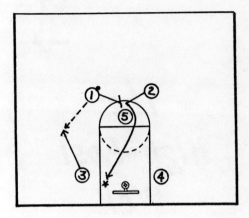

DIAGRAM 4-1

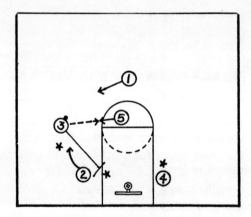

DIAGRAM 4-2

help on (2)'s initial cut or passing to (3) or (4) who have "shaped up" in the low-post areas on their respective sides of the free-throw lane.

2. To (1) who after his screen moved back toward the ball. In this event (3) again makes his pinching screen for (2) who again may be open for a jump shot. (Diagram 4-3)

The Outside Cut

This play starts the same way as the inside cut, but when guard (1) passes to (3) and comes over to form the wall, (2) fakes inside, cuts behind (1), and makes an outside cut on forward (3). (Diagram 4-4)

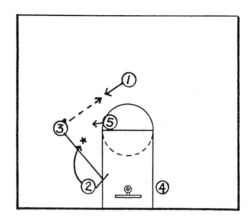

DIAGRAM 4-3

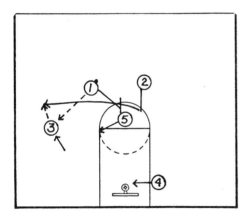

DIAGRAM 4-4

As (2) makes his outside cut, post man (5) moves toward the ball. Forward (3) then hands off to (2) and cuts over the high-post man to the area now occupied by forward (4). As soon as (2) receives the ball, the offside forward (4) moves across the foul lane for a possible pivot play in the ball-side low-post position. (Diagram 4-5) The post man (5) is instructed to set a definite screen on (3)'s defender as (3) hands the ball off to (1) and cuts over the post man.

This opens up the option of a possible cross-court lob pass from (2) to (3). (Diagram 4-5) Player (4) is considered the primary option as he shapes up for his one-on-one low-post play. Player (3), going over the top of the high-post man (5), has two functions. He is a threat because of the possible cross-court lob, but he also keeps (4)'s defensive man honest and almost disallows (4)'s defender from overplaying him. This defender must be aware of the lob pass and usually plays loose on (4) because of this possibility.

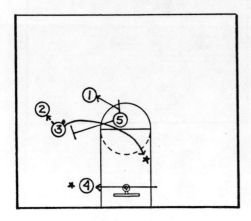

DIAGRAM 4-5

The Cross Play

This play is initiated when a guard passes the ball to the post man (5). As shown in Diagram 4-6, guard (2) passes the ball to the post man and again screens opposite for the guard (2). Guard (2) comes off this screen and crosses over for a possible jump shot.

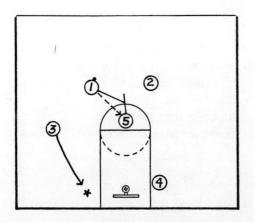

DIAGRAM 4-6

At the same time, forward (3), who was attempting to get open to receive a pass from (1), goes behind his defender and looks for a backdoor pass from the post man. (Diagram 4-6)

If (3) is not open, he keeps moving across the foul lane. Forward (4) waits and then cuts off (3) for a low-post play if he can get a pass from the post man. The post man (5) always has the option of a jump shot. (Diagram 4-7)

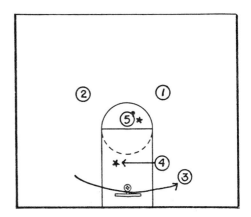

DIAGRAM 4-7

HIGH-POST WALL AUXILIARY PLAYS

Although the three previously described plays are our basic offense, at times we add others to give our offense more depth. Some of them follow.

Kas's Play

This play got its name because it was usually initiated by our playmaking guard, Kas Ioane. The play starts when guard (1) dribbles inside and hands the ball off to his forward (3). Forward (3) then comes outside with the ball and passes to guard (2). (Diagram 4-8)

Guard (2) then passes to his forward (4) and screens opposite for forward (3). Player (3) then fakes toward (2) and makes an inside cut to the ball-side low-post area. (Diagram 4-9)

111

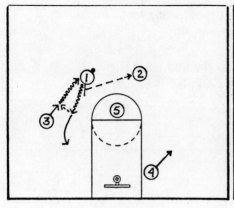

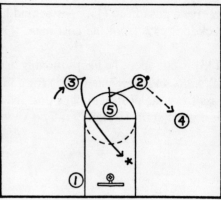

DIAGRAM 4-8   DIAGRAM 4-9

At the same time guard (1) goes up and makes a Headhunter screen on the high-post man's defender. The post man (5) wheels off the screen and looks for a cross-court lob pass from (4). (Diagram 4-10)

If (1)'s man switches, it results in a little man attempting to defend against an alley-oop pass to a big man.

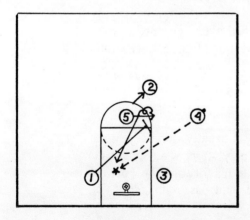

DIAGRAM 4-10

The Forward Fake

Any time our forwards receive the ball, our post man (5) moves toward them. As the season progresses, we give our forwards the

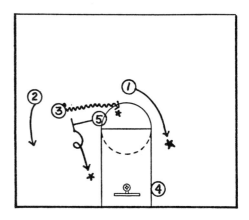

DIAGRAM 4-11

option of dribbling off the post. For example, Diagram 4-11 shows a pass being made to forward (3) and the outside-cut play developing. Forward (3) fakes the ball to guard (2) and dribbles off the post man (5).

Player (3) may jump shoot or pass off to the post man who has rolled following the screen.

Many times as (3) dribbles off the post, (1)'s defender will fall off and attempt to pick up (3). In anticipation of this, we have guard (1) drift away from the screen-and-roll play. As a result, (1) often gets an unmolested jump shot from a percentage area.

The Corner-Reverse Play

We run the corner play off both our inside-cut play and outside-cut play. It is keyed by a guard going to the ball-side corner and calling out ''Corner.''

When running our inside-cut play, the guard makes his slashing cut off the high post and goes directly to the corner. (Diagrams 4-12 and 4-13)

When running our outside-cut play, the forward fakes it to the guard (2) who continues to the corner. (Diagrams 4-14 and 4-15)

113

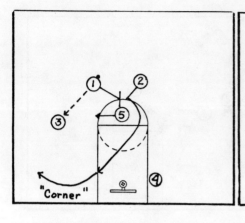

DIAGRAM 4-12

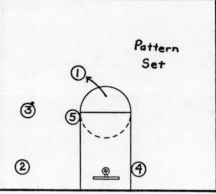

DIAGRAM 4-13

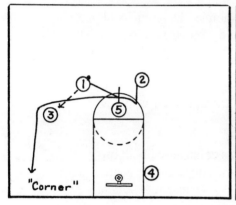

DIAGRAM 4-14

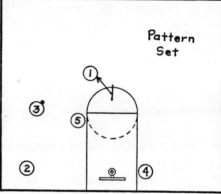

DIAGRAM 4-15

NOTE: This is the same key as the forward fake play so they both obviously cannot be part of your team techniques at the same time.

From this pattern set position, we can now run our corner-reverse play. Forward (3) reverses the ball to guard (1). The offside forward (4) sees or hears the key and moves up to screen for guard (1). (Diagram 4-16)

Player (1) dribbles off the screen and looks first for a jump shot. As soon as (1) picks up his dribble, the offside forward (3) makes

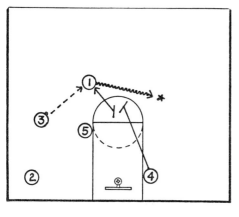

DIAGRAM 4-16

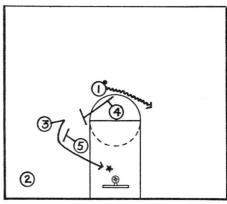

DIAGRAM 4-17

a change of direction and cuts off the post man (5) to the ball-side low-post area. (Diagram 4-17)

Player (4), who set the screen for guard (1), now moves to the offside high-post area. He, along with the post man (5), now form a double screen for guard (2), who changes direction and uses them as he comes out front. (Diagram 4-18)

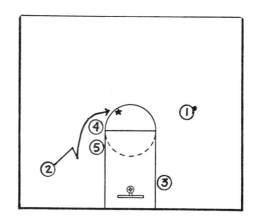

DIAGRAM 4-18

This play puts a lot of pressure on the defender guarding (2) to get over the double screen. To take advantage of this, a variation may be added. When forward (3) cuts off the post man (5) to the

115

ball-side low-post area and does not receive the ball, he clears to the ball-side corner. (Diagram 4-19)

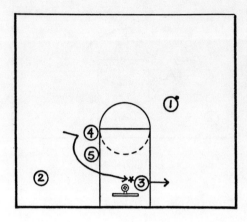

DIAGRAM 4-19

This tells (2) he may take advantage of his defender by starting to go over the double screen, thus setting up his man, and then spin off and go low for an easy layup. (Diagram 4-20)

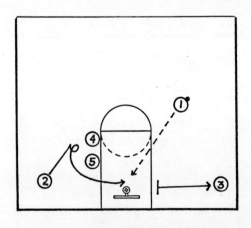

DIAGRAM 4-20

The Three-in-a-Row Play

This variation is run off the cross play. As the guards cross the midcourt line, they notice the forwards have pinched in and are in the high-post area. This tells the post man (5) to step forward

almost to the head of the key and receive a pass from guard (1).
(Diagram 4-21)

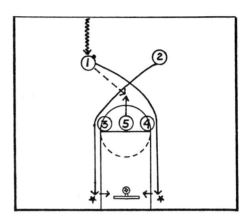

DIAGRAM 4-21

Guards (1) and (2) then crisscross off this very high post and also
utilize the screens set by the forwards on their respective sides.
Post man (5) pivots with the ball above his head and looks first to
drop the ball into either guard. If the guards are not open, they
slow down and both forwards roll toward the basket. Both guards
cross the free-throw lane in a very controlled manner and utilize
the rolling forwards as they rub off them for a possible short jump
shot. (Diagram 4-22)

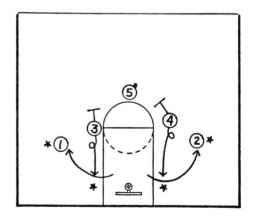

DIAGRAM 4-22

117

At times the defenders on forwards (3) and (4) may switch and leave them open in the layup slot area.

The Post-Opposite Play

This option is run from the inside-cut play. After the offside guard (2) cuts through to the ball-side low-post area, the post man (5) screens opposite for the offside forward (4). (Diagrams 4-23 and 4-24)

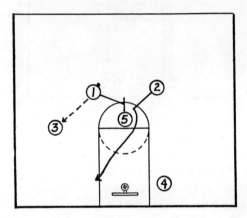

DIAGRAM 4-23

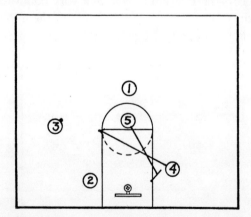

DIAGRAM 4-24

Forward (4) cuts to the ball. Guard (2) must watch this cut by (4) and clear to the corner if (4) gets the ball. If (4) is not open, the ball is passed to guard (1) out front. When this happens, the post

118

man (5) moves to the high-post area and (3) screens inside for (2). This gives guard (1) two options—(A) he may pass to (2) coming off (3)'s screen (Diagram 4-25), or (B) dribble off the post for a screen-and-roll play. (Diagram 4-26)

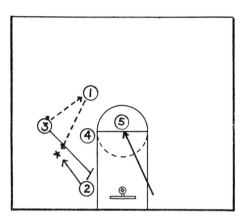

DIAGRAM 4-25

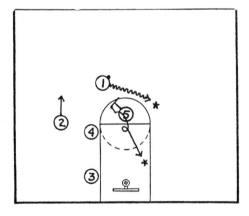

DIAGRAM 4-26

With the threat of a play being run to either side of the floor, defensive offside help is kept to a minimum.

The Double-Cut Series

Guard (1) passes to his forward (3) and forms a wall with the post man (5) for (2), the offside guard, who slashes off the wall to the ball-side low-post area (all this is per the guard-through play).

But, in this case, guard (1) also cuts through, down, and hooks around the forward (4) on his side. (Diagram 4-27)

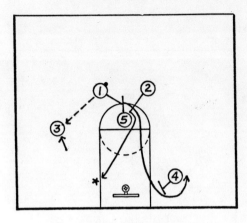

DIAGRAM 4-27

When this happens, forward (3) passes quickly to the post man (5) and pinches in to screen for guard (2). (Diagram 4-28)

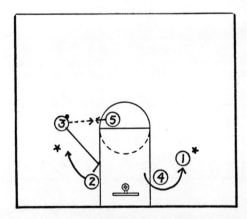

DIAGRAM 4-28

The post man (5) may now pass to guards (1) or (2) who have hooked around their forwards or to their forwards in the respective low-post areas. When the pass is made inside to the forwards, it usually results in a power layup. If the pass is made to a guard as shown in Diagram 4-29, guard (1) may now:

1. Jump shoot if he is open.
2. Throw a cross-court pass to the other guard (2).

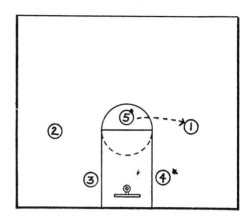

DIAGRAM 4-29

NOTE: For years the cross-court pass was discouraged but now is considered an effective weapon against zones and sagging man-to-man defenses.

3. Pass to forward (4) in the ball-side low-post area for what will often result in a one-on-one pivot play.

From here, we are in pattern set and either of two variations may be run.

The Offside Post Rotation. If player (1) finds none of his first three options open, he may now look to the high-post area. Upon passing to player (1), the post man (5) followed his rotation rule, which is: *When passing to either of the guards who occupy wing positions, rotate to the offside low-post area.* The man from the offside low-post area then replaces the post man in the high-post position. (See players (3) and (5) in Diagram 4-30.)

Using the Double-Cut Series Against Zone Defenses. It is very functional when you can get the ball into the high-post area against zone defenses, so guard (1) is encouraged to get the ball to (3). Once (3) gets the ball, he may jump shoot or pass to either of the men in the layup slots. If neither of these situations occurs, he reverses the ball to guard (2) and he and player (4) make their offside rotation. (Diagram 4-31) The same options are now available to guard (2).

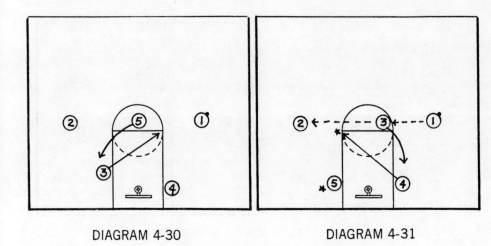

DIAGRAM 4-30   DIAGRAM 4-31

When an offside post rotation has been made and a cutter has gone to the high-post area, he is not always clear. When he finds himself covered, he must step out to the head of the key in order to receive the ball from a guard. (Diagram 4-32)

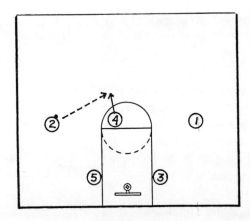

DIAGRAM 4-32

He may now pass to either guard and make another offside rotation, jump shoot if open, or hit the inside men for power layups.

The Overload Variation.   If after the double cut by the guards has been made an overload is desired, it will be keyed by the onside low-post man who is forward (4) in Diagrams 4-33 and 4-34.

122

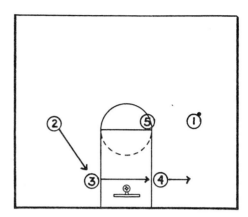

DIAGRAM 4-33

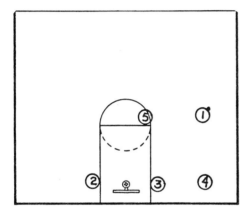

DIAGRAM 4-34

Player (4) cuts to the ball-side corner. This tells the offside offensive men to slide in that direction and fill the vacated spots, and results in an overload that will continue until the ball is reversed to the other side by way of the post man.

NOTE: Once this happens, an offside post rotation will follow a now overload if the now onside low-post man so desires. (See Diagrams 4-35, 4-36 and 4-37.)

The Shuffle Phase

The Shuffle phase is a five-man continuity that may be run from either the inside-cut or outside-cut play. It is very useful when your post man is being dominated by his defensive man.

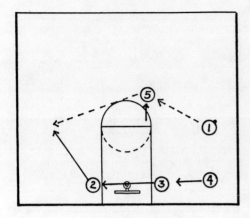

DIAGRAM 4-35

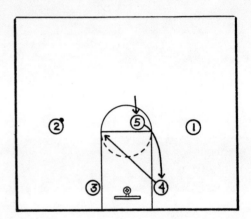

DIAGRAM 4-36

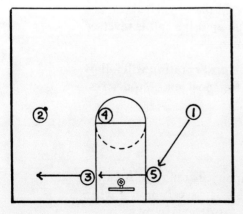

DIAGRAM 4-37

124

The Inside Cut. The inside-cut play starts as before with the initiating guard passing to his forward and forming a wall for the offside guard. The offside guard then cuts off the high post on a slash cut to the low-post area as before. (Diagram 4-38)

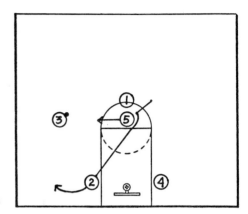

DIAGRAM 4-38

From here, the Shuffle option begins. The forward with the ball (3) passes the ball to the remaining guard out front (1) who reverses it to the offside forward (4). Forward (3) then makes a Shuffle cut off the post. (Diagram 4-39)

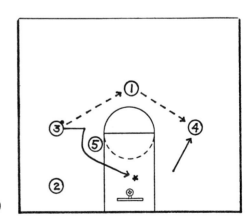

DIAGRAM 4-39

The post man (5) then drops down and screens for (2) who cuts to the ball side of the free-throw line to become tne new post man. (Diagram 4-40)

125

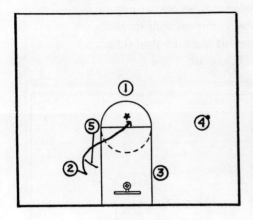

DIAGRAM 4-40

If neither (3) nor (2) is open, (4) dribbles toward (1), passes to him, and becomes the first cutter when (1) reverses the ball to (5). After (4) has cut, (2) drops down and screens for (3) and the offense has been turned over again. (Diagrams 4-41 and 4-42)

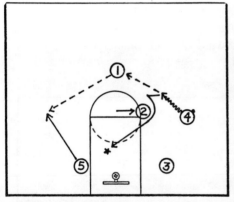

DIAGRAM 4-41

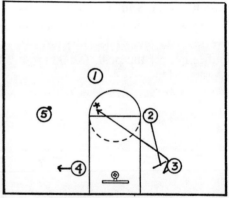

DIAGRAM 4-42

The Outside Cut. The outside cut begins as before with the onside guard (1) passing to his forward (3) and forming the wall for the offside guard (2). The offside guard makes an outside cut and gets the ball back from (3). Forward (3) then cuts over the post man (5) for the possible lob pass and the offside forward comes across the low post. (Diagrams 4-43 and 4-44)

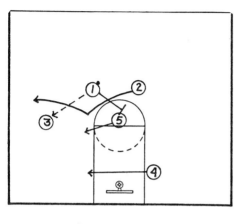

DIAGRAM 4-43

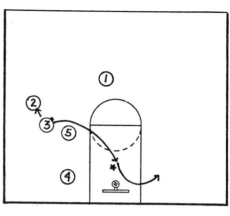

DIAGRAM 4-44

The ball is then reversed from (2) to (1) to (3) and the two Shuffle options are run. (Diagrams 4-45 and 4-46)

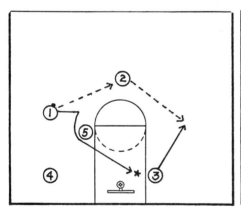

DIAGRAM 4-45

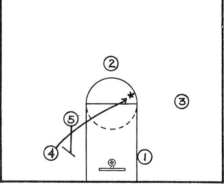

DIAGRAM 4-46

The Cross Play. When running the Shuffle phase, we invert our guards and forwards on any pass to the post. That is accomplished by the guards coming down and screening for the forward on their respective sides. (Diagram 4-47)

It is possible for the forwards to be open off these screens or the

127

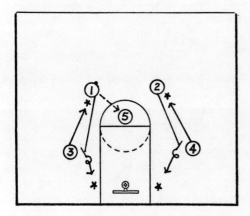

DIAGRAM 4-47

guards rolling to the inside. However, the main thing that has happened is that the guards and forwards have changed positions and the defense is presented with an entirely new picture.

This Shuffle phase gives the small team a method of reshuffling the opposition's defensive assignments before running their offense.

UTILIZING THE HIGH-POST WALL OFFENSE VERSUS ZONE DEFENSES

Splitting the Zone

This High-Post Wall Offense may be run against zones and allows a team to split, overload, overshift, penetrate, and screen them.

Since the offense was a two-man front, it naturally splits the odd front (1-3-1, 1-2-2 and 3-2) zones. (Diagrams 4-48, 4-49 and 4-50)

Against even front (2-3 and 2-1-2) zones, the offensive guards are played wide apart (at least as wide as the free-throw lane). This spreads their front two defenders and makes it easy to get the ball to the high-post man. (Diagram 4-51) Also, on each of the three plays, a guard cuts through. This leaves the even front zone with two men out front against one offensive man and, in effect, splits them. (Diagrams 4-52 and 4-53)

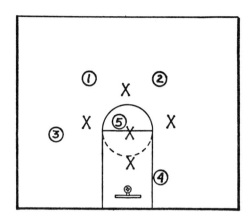

DIAGRAM 4-48

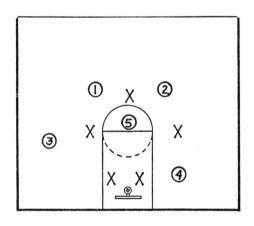

DIAGRAM 4-49

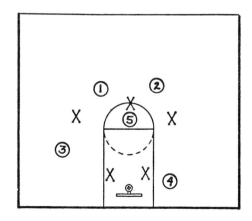

DIAGRAM 4-50

129

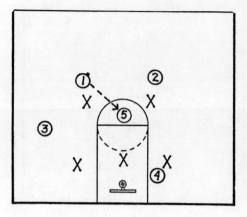

DIAGRAM 4-51

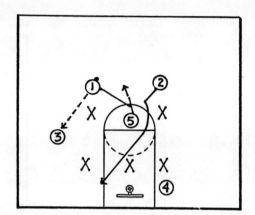

DIAGRAM 4-52

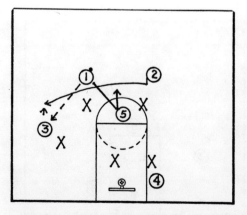

DIAGRAM 4-53

130

The Inside-Cut Play

When the onside guard (1) passes to his forward (3), the offside guard (2) cuts through to the ball-side low-post area. (Diagrams 4-54 and 4-55)

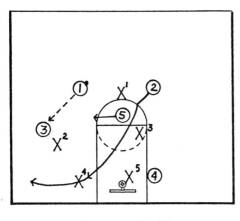

DIAGRAM 4-54

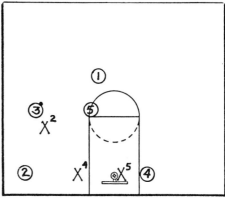

DIAGRAM 4-55

Against zones, the cutting guard (2) does not stop, but continues to the ball-side corner. (Diagram 4-56) Once this has happened, the lead back man (X^4) must respect (2) and slide in that direction.

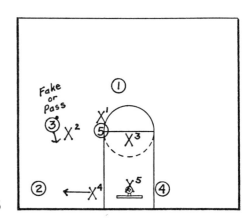

DIAGRAM 4-56

131

From here the following things may happen:

A. If (3) sees that (X^5) has not trailed (X^4) close enough, he can hit his post man (5) with a lob lead pass, which may give him a power layup. (Diagram 4-57)

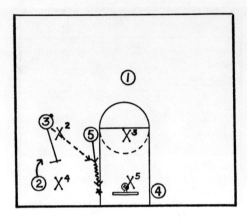

DIAGRAM 4-57

B. If (X^5) does slide over eight feet behind (X^4), a pass to the post man (5) may leave (4) open in the offside layup slot. (Diagram 4-58)

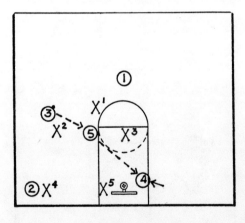

DIAGRAM 4-58

Both of these plays are facilitated if the forward will fake to the guard in the corner before passing to the post. Whenever (3) passes to the post, he always screens for guard (2) as per the man-to-man play.

C. Forward (3) may pass back to guard (1) just as he had in the man-to-man option. (Diagram 4-59) Guard (1) then takes one dribble toward the other side. When this happens, the former onside defensive wing man (X^2) knows he is now to sag into rebound position. (Diagram 4-60)

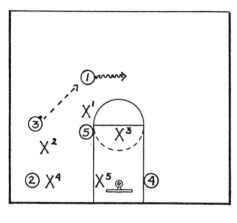

DIAGRAM 4-59

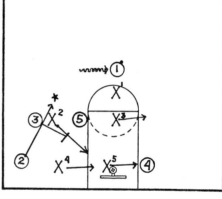

DIAGRAM 4-60

From here (1) fakes a pass to (4) and (3) moves in to screen (X^2). Player (2) takes advantage of this screen and comes out for an unmolested jump shot. (Diagram 4-61)

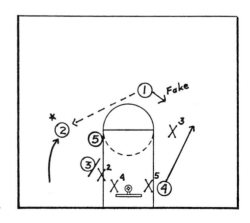

DIAGRAM 4-61

D. In the event (2) is not open, the offense is now back in its original alignment, and if (1) tries to catch the zone overshifted by passing to (4), the same play may be run again. (Diagrams 4-62 and 4-63)

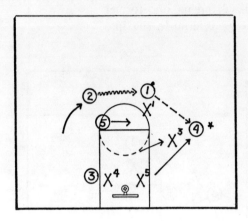

DIAGRAM 4-62

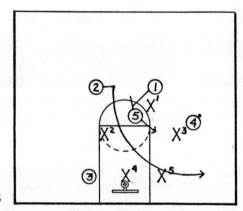

DIAGRAM 4-63

The Outside-Cut Play

The onside guard (1) passes to his forward (3) and the offside guard (2) makes his outside cut. (Diagram 4-64)

When running this play against man-to-man, the offside forward (4) is told not to come across the lane until (3) hands off to (2).

134

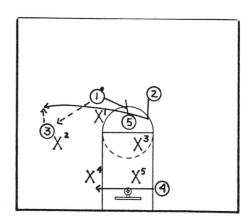

DIAGRAM 4-64

But against zones, the offside forward comes across as soon as guard (2) makes his cut. (See Diagram 4-64.) He also does not stop in the ball-side low post, but instead continues to the ball-side corner. (Diagram 4-65)

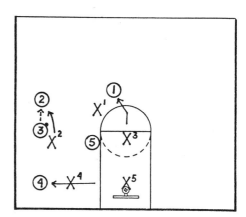

DIAGRAM 4-65

After (3) has handed off to (2), he makes his cut over the top of the post man (5).

NOTE: The cross-court lob pass cannot be worked against zones.

From here the following options may occur:

135

A. Player (2) may reverse the ball to (3) by way of (1) and catch the zone overshifted. (Diagram 4-66)

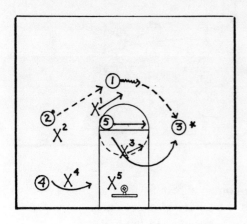

DIAGRAM 4-66

B. If (2) passes to the post man (5), the post man looks for both forwards (3) and (4) in the layup slots.

When the pass is made from guard (2) to the post man (5), the cut to the layup slot area on his side works very much like a backdoor play. (Diagram 4-67)

This works especially well if (2) will fake a pass to (4) and then pass to the post.

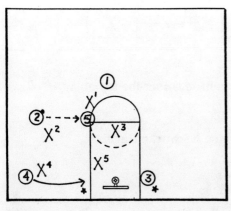

DIAGRAM 4-67

C. If (2) does pass to (4) in the corner, the post slides down and (4) attempts to get the ball to him. (Diagram 4-68)

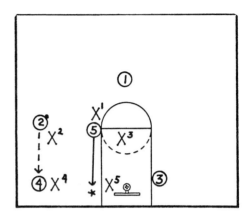

DIAGRAM 4-68

D. If (2) dribbles out front, a new play is run.

The Cross Play

When a guard passes to the high-post man (5), the guards and forwards cross and try to find a hole in the zone. (Diagram 4-69)

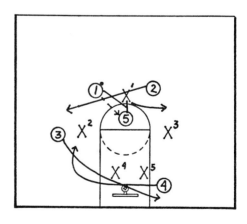

DIAGRAM 4-69

137

TEACHING THE HIGH-POST WALL OFFENSE

Personnel

Coaching Points

Initial Spacing. When teaching this play, the first thing we stress is spacing. The guards are to be as wide apart as the foul lane, the high-post man in the middle of the lane, and the two forwards are in tight in their respective layup slots. We want the ball-side forward to break as high as the free-throw line extended to receive the pass from his guard. If his cut starts from the ball-side layup slot and he breaks out in a diagonal cut, it is difficult for his defender to stay with him without being very vulnerable to a backdoor-type cut. The forwards are taught to receive the ball with their inside foot forward. This permits them to pivot on their outside foot which is trailing and, as a result, their initial range of movement is greatly extended. The offside forward is told that he is the primary rebounder and must do what he can to gain an advantageous position on his defender while the play progresses. The post man is in the middle of the foul lane and just above the free-throw line.

This offense is versatile in that it can be used either by a team that lacks a big man or a team that is blessed with three big men. The ideal personnel would be the following.

The *guards* would be taller than average and have the ability to post their defenders. The inside-cut play sends the guards through to the low-post area on the ball side and if they can set up and receive a pass from the forward, this is a very high percentage area and many fouls are drawn on pivot shots.

The *high-post player* ideally would have a high percentage jump shot from the free-throw line, be a more-than-adequate feeder, and have the desire to storm the boards from the high-post area when a shot is missed.

The *forwards* do most of their scoring from the low-post area, so it would help if they possessed the ability to score on pivot plays and were taller than average.

The Inside-Cut Play

Most teams overplay the forwards. One of the blessings of a High-Post Wall Offense is that the forwards have a lot of room to get open to receive the ball and a clear path to the basket once they have it. Because of this attribute, two moves should be taught to the forwards to combat overplay:

The Straight Backdoor. When the forward makes his diagonal cut out to the free-throw line extended and is overplayed so strongly that he cannot receive the ball, he should key the back-door play by taking a not-too-fast step toward the basket. This will, in most cases, cause his defender to drop back slightly. At this point, a signal may be given to the guard that the forward plans to backdoor. The one we have used is for the forward to extend his outside arm and pat his chest with his inside hand. By then, the defender is tight again and the forward takes a jab step forward, pushes off this front foot, goes behind his defensive man and receives a lob or bounce pass for a layup shot.

The Reverse Pivot. If the forward, when coming out to meet the ball, will use a jump stop, he can pivot on either foot. This allows him to wheel to the outside and go all the way to the basket upon receiving the ball.

After the forward (3) receives the ball, the offside guard (2) cuts to the low-post area. Here, again, the guard's first option is to post his man. To do this, he must establish a strong position by lowering his center of gravity. From here he must learn to read his defender. In most cases, the defensive man will overplay him to one side. The offensive man takes advantage of this by raising the elbow closest to the defensive man shoulder high, and extending the arm furthest from his defender. This fends off his defender, gives the passer a target and the receiver a potential quick move to the basket when he catches the ball. We also tell him to get some part of his body closer to the basket than his defender. This can be his far arm or back foot.

If the pivot option does not develop, the forward may pass to either the high-post man (5) or the other guard (1) out front and

139

come down and make a pinching-type screen for the inside guard (2). When the ball is passed to the high post and the forward (3) starts down to screen, at times the inside guard's defender will anticipate the screen and beat his man over it. When this happens, guard (2) should fake coming off the screen, cut back to the layup area, and receive a pass from the post man for a power layup shot. (Diagram 4-70)

When, as in most cases, the guard (2) does use the screen and comes out, the screener (3) must realize that he, too, is a scoring option. When he sets his screen, he should face the man with the ball as much as possible and keep his hands in a ready position. Many times a switch is made between the defenders of (3) and (1), and (3) is left open. The action of (3) passing to the high post and pinching for (1) usually draws the attention of the defense. Very often the offside forward's (4) defender will slide over to help. Because of this, the high-post man is instructed to look for the offside forward and the offside forward is told that as soon as the high-post man looks at him, he should move into the lane and post his defender. The high-post man (5) may now shoot, pass to either of the posting forwards or the guard coming off the pinching screen. If nothing develops, he may return the ball to the safety valve guard (1) out front.

The Outside Cut

Many times when the forward (3) receives the ball, the defender on the guard making the outside cut will stay with him and make it difficult for the return pass to be made. When this happens, (2) must make a strong move toward the basket before making the outside cut. If the defender fails to respect this move, (2) may get an easy layup; if he does back up, (2) may be able to receive the return pass from (3).

NOTE: When the guard making the outside cut is being pressured, another option may be run to loosen up his defender. It is what is usually called the Dayton play. As (3) receives the ball and (2) comes outside, (3) passes the ball to the high-post man and closes the gate on (2)'s defender by making a slight

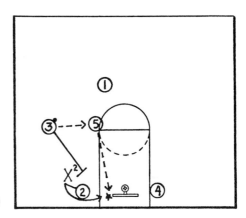

DIAGRAM 4-70

back pivot. Guard (2) cuts close to (3), rubs off his defender, and continues to the basket to receive a pass for a layup from the high-post man (5). (Diagrams 4-71 and 4-72) This is a play that may be called during a time-out period.

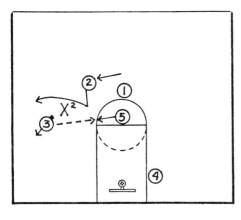

DIAGRAM 4-71   DIAGRAM 4-72

From here, the keys to this play are:

1. The high-post man must set a *definite* screen on (3)'s defender.
2. When (3) cuts over the screen, he must not make a rainbow-type cut but must cut to the basket in the offside layup slot.

141

3. Guard (2) must be taught that the forward coming cross the low-post area is in great position to score. If he is open, get him the ball.

NOTE: If (3)'s defender continually goes inside of the screen, we use the following counter we call "seal."

When the offside forward comes across the lane, he goes directly to (3)'s defender and, in effect, screens him for the second time. This often allows the lob pass to be thrown to (3). (Diagrams 4-73 and 4-74)

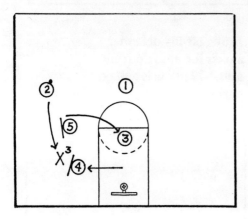

DIAGRAM 4-73

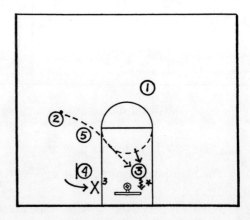

DIAGRAM 4-74

The Cross Play

This play is run primarily to take the pressure off the forward attempting to receive the ball to start the play. This play must be timed well to be effective.

The guard (1) making the pass to start the play must first fake to the forward (3) to force his defender into an overplay position. When the pass is made to the post, it should be a bounce pass. Player (3) should make his backdoor move as the ball hits the floor. Upon receiving the ball, the post man looks first for this backdoor man. If (3) is not open, he clears low to the opposite side of the lane.

The offside forward (4) now swings across the lane looking for a high-post-to-low-post pass. This puts a lot of pressure on (4)'s defender and, if the high-post man (5) is a clever faker and passer, often results in close-in, power layup shots for (4).

The guards cross to keep their men busy while the two inside options are explored. At times the guards will get open, but usually the play goes inside.

DRILLS TO TEACH THE HIGH-POST WALL OFFENSE

The Breakdown Drill

These drills are run with no defense. One play is taken at a time. Each option is run repeatedly with each member of the team taking his turn at his position.

The Recognition Drill

The guards call the play with their pass and cut and the other players attempt to recognize the play and run it through to a shot option.

143

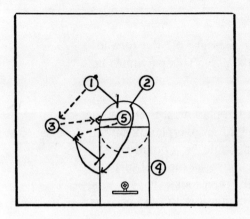

DIAGRAM 4-75
Inside cut

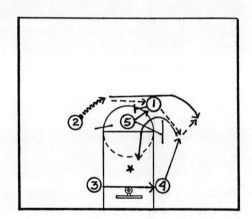

DIAGRAM 4-76
Outside cut

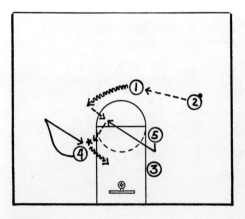

DIAGRAM 4-77
Cross play

144

The Three-Times-Around Drill

The offense is run as a continuity. All three plays are run with the ball coming out front after each of the first two plays and a shot being taken on the third play, for example. (Diagrams 4-75, 4-76 and 4-77)

The Isolation Drill

All three plays may be run. Defensive players are placed on the two guards. The guards must score by way of the scoring options. New offensive players come in after each play. The defensive men must stop three plays in a row to get off of defense. The same drill is then run with the defenders on the forwards.

5

The Multi-Option Continuity

Modern defenses pressure on the ball side and jam the middle from the offside. The following offense utilizes the front court from sideline to sideline and makes it more difficult for the defense to do its job. The fact that it is a continuity offense also allows the offensive players access to the scoring area.

THE MULTI-OPTION CONTINUITY VERSUS MAN-TO-MAN

The pattern begins with guard (1) dribbling toward the sideline on his forward (3)'s side. As soon as (1) throws the ball to forward (3), the offside forward (4) makes a change of direction and cuts off the post man (5) and into the ball-side layup slot. (Diagram 5-1)

As soon as guard (1) passes to forward (3), he screens opposite for the other guard (2). This gives forward (3) the option of passing to (4) in the post area or guard (2) moving toward him for a possible jump shot. (Diagram 5-2) Since neither (4) nor (2) was open, (4) continues to the ball-side corner where he receives a pass from forward (3). (Diagram 5-3)

Forward (3) then cuts across the free-throw lane and forms a moving screen for the post man (5) who uses (3) and attempts to shape up in the pivot area.

147

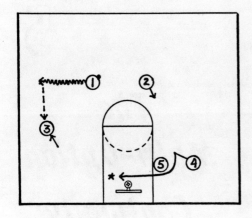

DIAGRAM 5-1

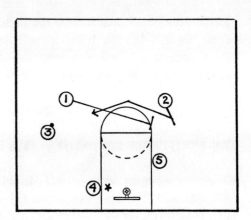

DIAGRAM 5-2

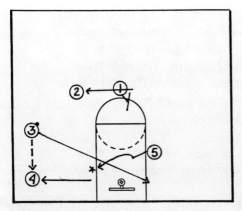

DIAGRAM 5-3

148

If the post man is not open, forward (4) passes the ball to guard
(2) who reverses the ball to guard (1). Guard (1) dribbles toward
the offside and the continuity is begun on the other side. (Diagrams 5-4 and 5-5)

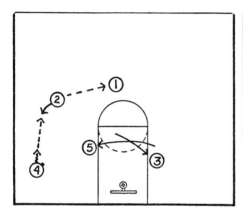

DIAGRAM 5-4

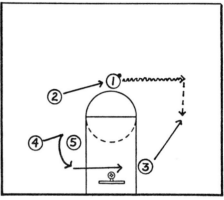

DIAGRAM 5-5

In this case, the now offside forward (4) again cuts off the post
man (5) and in to the ball-side low-post area. (Diagram 5-5) The
ball-side guard (1) screens away for the offside guard (2). The
forward cutting off the post still is not open so he clears to the
corner. (Diagram 5-6)

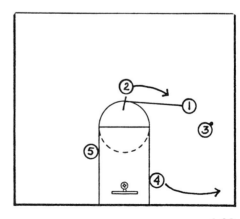

DIAGRAM 5-6

But this time (3) feels the guard (2) moving toward him is open, so he passes to him. When forward (3) makes this pass, he again goes across to screen for the post man (5). Guard (2) may now:

1. Go all the way to the basket if he can.
2. Jump shoot.
3. Stop and look for the post man coming across the lane.

The post man (5) must watch the guard and not take his play away from him. As soon as guard (2) is stopped, the post man swings to the ball-side post area. (Diagram 5-7)

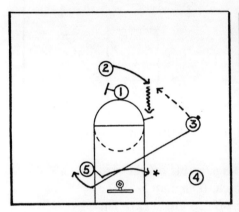

DIAGRAM 5-7

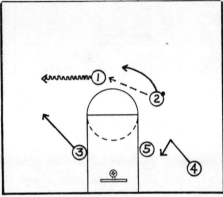

DIAGRAM 5-8

If the post man (5) is not open, (2) stops, pivots, and reverses the ball to guard (1) who dribbles to the opposite side to continue the play. (Diagram 5-8)

Players' Rules

Following are the players' rules by position.

Guards. The *lead guard* will dribble toward his forward, make a penetration pass and screen opposite for the trailing guard.

The *trailing guard* will come off the screen, look for a pass from the forward with the ball, look first for his own scoring options, look to the post coming across the lane and, if nothing happens, reverse the ball to the other guard.

Forwards.   The *ball-side forward* will receive a pass from his guard, look for the offside forward coming across, look for the guard moving toward him, and look for the offside forward clearing to the corner. After he makes any of these possible passes, he always does the same thing—he moves across the lane and forms a moving screen for the post man.

The *offside forward* makes a change of direction and cuts off the post man to the ball-side post area; if he is not open, he clears to the ball-side corner. If he receives a pass from the ball-side corner, he looks first for the post coming across and second for the guard moving toward him.

Post Man.   The *post man* forms a screen for the offside forward, waits for the ball-side forward to pass to the guard coming off the screen or the clearing forward in the corner. After the ball-side forward makes his pass and moves across the lane, the post man uses him to get open in the ball-side low-post area.

The Split Rule

Whenever a man cutting to the post receives a pass, the passer splits the post with the man nearest the baseline. Two examples of this rule in action are:

1.   When the onside forward (3) has the ball and the offside forward (4) cuts off the post man (5), (3) passes to him. Since at this time there is no one in the corner, the nearest player to the baseline is the guard moving toward (3), so he splits the post with him. (Diagram 5-9)
2.   In this case, the ball-side forward (3) has decided the cutting offside forward is not open, and the forward has cleared to the corner. Forward (3) passes the ball to the guard (2) moving toward him, and screens opposite for the post man. (Diagram 5-10)

151

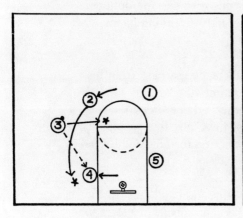

DIAGRAM 5-9

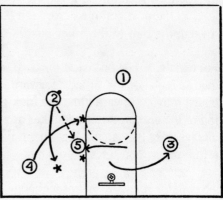

DIAGRAM 5-10

Guard (2) passes to the man in the post area and splits the post with the man closest to the baseline (4). Again, the rule is: *When you pass to a man in the post area, split the post with the man closest to the baseline.*

NOTE: The basic play is usually initiated on the weak side. When it is started on the strong side, the post man (5) swings opposite on the dribble by the lead guard. (Diagram 5-11)

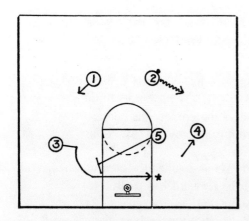

DIAGRAM 5-11

From there, lead guard (2) passes to forward (4) and the same options prevail.

MULTI-OPTION CONTINUITY AUXILIARY PLAYS

During the course of the Multi-Option Continuity, there are plays that can be incorporated without destroying the flow of the pattern.

The Cross-Court Lob Play

At times during the continuity, the post man (5) will key a cross-court lob play by coming across the lane at the same time or even before the offside forward (4). (Diagram 5-12)

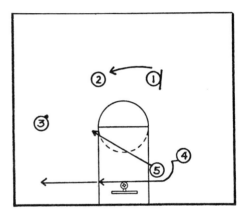

DIAGRAM 5-12

When this happens, the forward (3) with the ball passes to the forward who has cut to the post and then clears to the corner. After this pass, (3) goes over top of the post and to the offside layup slot. The post man (5) sets a definite screen on (3)'s man. Now player (4) may lob the pass cross-court to (3). (Diagram 5-13)

If (3) is not open, (4) can take a dribble toward (2), the guard moving toward him, and reverse the ball from (2) to (1). Player (1) may now dribble to the sideline and run the play on the other side. (Diagrams 5-14 and 5-15)

NOTE: The post man (5) should roll after his screen of (3) in the event of a switch.

153

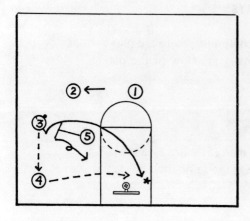

DIAGRAM 5-13

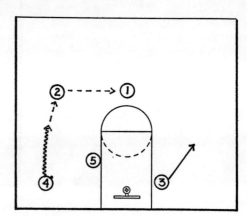

DIAGRAM 5-14

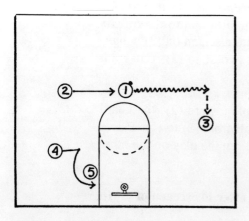

DIAGRAM 5-15

The continuity is now run on the opposite side.

The Corner Play

This is a very simple play that is often very effective. When the onside forward (3) passes to the clearing forward (4) in the corner and goes through, the post man (5) comes to the ball side. For the corner play, the forward with the ball (4) hesitates and the post sets a blind screen on his man.

The corner man dribbles off this screen, looks first for a jump shot and then for the post man (5) rolling. (Diagrams 5-16, 5-17)

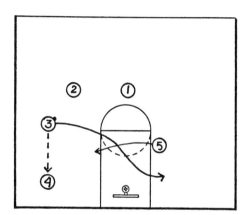

DIAGRAM 5-16

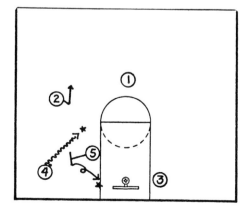

DIAGRAM 5-17

155

Guard (2) must see this play developing and stay clear of it. If neither phase of this screen-and-roll play develops, (4) bounce passes directly to the trailing guard who dribbles to his sideline and the continuity goes on. (Diagram 5-18)

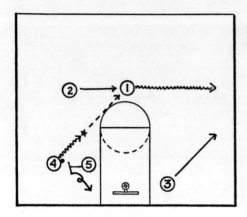

DIAGRAM 5-18

The Wall Play

When guard (1) passes to his forward (3) and screens opposite for guard (2), the offside forward does not come across the lane. This tells (2), the guard coming off the screen, to continue his cut to the basket. The first option is for (3) to pass to him for a layup shot. (Diagram 5-19) If this does not develop, (2) continues his

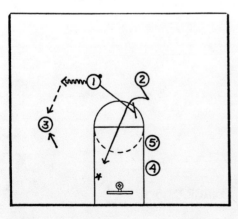

DIAGRAM 5-19

cut and goes around the double screen (wall) formed by the post man (5) and forward (4). As soon as (2) comes around the wall, the post man swings across the lane. (Diagram 5-20)

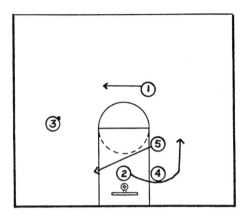

DIAGRAM 5-20

In the event (3) passes to the post man (5), he splits the post with (3). (Diagram 5-21)

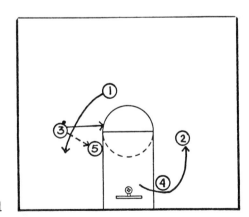

DIAGRAM 5-21

If the post man is not open, (3) reverses the ball by way of guard (1) to guard (2) who cut behind the wall.

If (2) does not have a shot, he dribbles toward the sideline and the continuity goes on. (Diagrams 5-22 and 5-23)

157

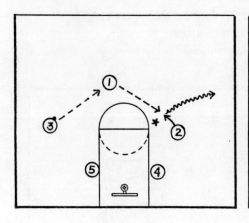

DIAGRAM 5-22

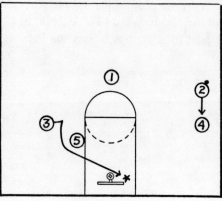

DIAGRAM 5-23

THE MULTI-OPTION CONTINUITY VERSUS ZONE DEFENSES

Rotating Front

When guard (1) dribbles toward the sideline to start the offense, the zone defense is at once presented with a unique problem: Does point man (X^1) follow the dribbler? We exclusively played zone defense at Eastern Montana College for nine seasons and our rule was: *If the man with the ball dribbles, you must stay with him until he is stopped.* This simple move by itself would have rotated our point man out of his zone and left the remaining offensive guard open. (Diagrams 5-24 and 5-25)

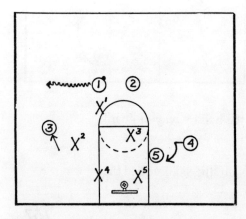

DIAGRAM 5-24

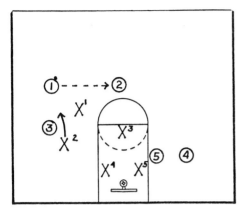

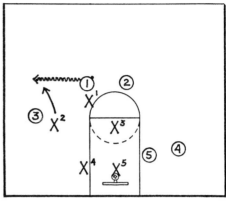

DIAGRAM 5-25   DIAGRAM 5-26

If the defensive wing man (X^2) comes up to cover (1), it leaves offensive forward (3) open. (Diagram 5-26)

Once the defense has been placed at a disadvantage by this seldom-seen move, guard (1) passes to his forward (3) and screens opposite for guard (2). If the defensive front collapses, this screen may be fairly effective. Now that forward (3) has the ball, the offside forward (4) cuts to the ball-side low-post area. If he is not open, he clears to the ball-side corner.

Forward Options

Forward (3) has the following options:

A. He may pass to the forward in the ball-side corner, make a cut toward the basket looking for the ball, and then clear to the offside. (Diagram 5-27) The forward in the corner, (4), may now:

1. Shoot, if open.
2. Pass to the cutting forward. (Diagram 5-27)
3. Pass to the post man (5) (who is keyed by the forward (3)'s cut) in the center of the zone at the ¾ post area. (Diagram 5-28)
4. Get the ball to the guard (2) cutting toward him. (Diagram 5-29)

159

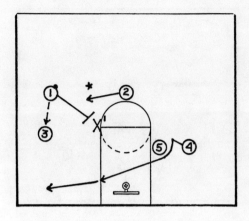

DIAGRAM 5-27

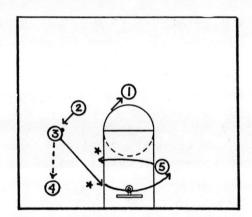

DIAGRAM 5-28

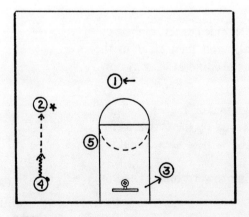

DIAGRAM 5-29

The guard (2) with the ball may now shoot or reverse the ball to the other guard who dribbles to the opposite sideline to start the pattern again.

B. Forward (3) may pass to guard (2) coming toward him off the screen by (1). (Diagram 5-30) When forward (3) does this, he again cuts to the basket and clears to the offside. By now (4) has cut to the ball-side corner and (3)'s cut has keyed the post man to come to the ¾ post area. (Diagram 5-31)

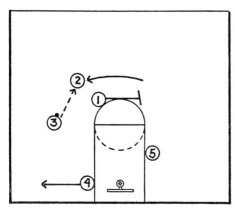

DIAGRAM 5-30

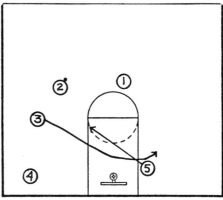

DIAGRAM 5-31

Guard Options

Guard (2) may now:

1. Shoot, if he is open.
2. Pass to the post man (5) in the center of the zone.
3. Pass to (4) in the corner and take advantage of the overload situation. This overload will continue until the ball is passed to guard (1) and he decides to dribble away to start another offensive phase. (Diagrams 5-32 and 5-33)

TEACHING THE MULTI-OPTION CONTINUITY

This offense is designed for a team with a strong potential inside game. Most of the options are in the pivot area.

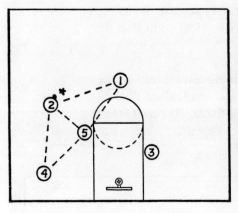

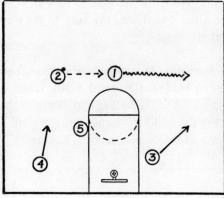

DIAGRAM 5-32   DIAGRAM 5-33

Personnel

Guards. The guards can be small, but they must be the playmaker type. They should have the ability to score on a ten- to fifteen-foot jump shot. This offense also demands that they dribble well with either hand.

Forwards. The forwards take most of their shots with their backs to the basket. Actually, this offense would allow a coach to play three pivot man type players at once. This is quite an attribute for college teams where, in many cases, the forwards played the pivot position in high school.

Post Man. Here is where the real strength of this offense can be pointed out. It is an offshoot of the reverse-action offense, which is an offense that interchanges its three inside men. The reverse-action offense is very difficult to defense because it has continuous offside screens. Its one weakness is that the post man is very often playing a forward position. The Multi-Option Continuity features the same offside screens, but keeps the post man inside at all times. He is either in the ball-side post area and is a scoring option, or he is in the offside post area, which is usually considered the primary rebounding area. This means the team with the big, talented pivot man can utilize this offense, which will (a) keep him in the post area, (b) keep the defense moving and involved in defensing the offside screens, and (c) give him plenty of room to work because this offense takes the defense from sideline to sideline.

Coaching Points

Cutting Off the Post Man

After the weakside guard has initiated the play by dribbling toward his forward and passing to him, the offside forward cuts off the post man. The offside forward should cut below the post man at least seventy-five percent of the time because this type of cut is much more difficult to defense. When he makes the low cut, there is a point at which only one of the two defenders involved can see the entire play. When the cutter goes over the top, the two defenders on the play can both see the play at all times.

Another point to remember when running this offside screen is that if a switch is made or if the post man's defender plays very loose to cover the forward's cut, a cross-court pass may be thrown from the ball-side forward (3) to the post man (5) for an easy jump shot. (Diagram 5-34)

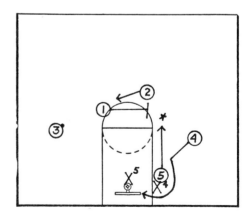

DIAGRAM 5-34

As the offside forward (4) comes off the post man's screen, he should slow down when he is basket high and stop when he gets just outside the foul lane for a one-thousand-one verbal count.

When this time is over, he should clear to the corner. (Diagram 5-35)

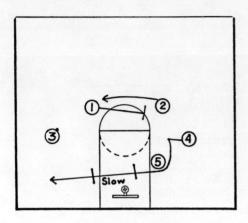

DIAGRAM 5-35

The Moving Screen

After (4) has cleared to the corner, (3) passes the ball to him and cuts toward the post man. The success of this moving screen will depend on how the post man uses it. If his defender is playing off of him, he must move toward the free-throw line. If his defender reacts to this move, the post man (5) then moves back to his original position and, in many cases, his defender will come with him. (Diagrams 5-36 and 5-37)

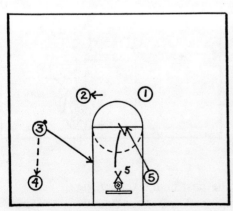

DIAGRAM 5-36

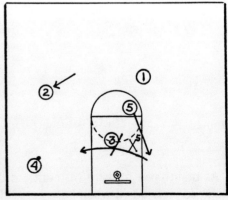

DIAGRAM 5-37

If his defender ignores his cut to the free-throw line, he may be open for a jump shot.

The Guards' Crossing Action

When the playmaking guard (1) dribbles toward his forward, the offside guard (2) must move away from the play and keep his man busy. After guard (1) has passed to his forward and come across to screen for him, (2) must still time his cut and be sure not to get to the ball side too soon. The best way for the offside guard (2) to time this is to make a move to the ball, then, as he sees guard (1) coming toward him, make a sharp move away from the ball and then come off (1)'s screen after guard (1) has stopped. On occasion when his man is completely beaten, he should go all the way through and run the wall play. If (2)'s man gets over the screen prematurely, it also might be a wise move for (2) to go backdoor. If he isn't open on this move, the wall play is run. (Diagram 5-38)

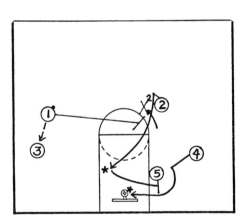

DIAGRAM 5-38

DRILLS TO TEACH THE MULTI-OPTION CONTINUITY

One-on-One in the Post

The success of this offense will be determined for the most part by the ability of the three inside men to score in the pivot area. A very functional drill for this offense is to designate three passers.

One plays at the head of the key, one plays at the left forward position, and the other at the right forward position. The remaining players are in a line under the basket and out-of-bounds. One player is chosen to be the defensive man. The first man in the line starts on offense. The idea is for one of the three passers to get the ball in to the offensive man on a two-second count, and if he cannot, move the ball on to the next passer. The offensive player learns to move to the ball, to use his body to get open, to maintain an advantage once he has acquired one, and to take advantage of his defender's overplay position in order to get an easy shot. In short, he must learn to read the pivot defense and counter it. If the offensive man scores, he goes to the end of the line. If he does not, he goes on defense and the former defender goes to the end of the line.

Forwards' Two-on-Two

Because this offense is a continuity that depends on the guard being able to make a penetrating pass to the forward on his side, much time should be spent on this phase. The forwards' two-on-two drill is set up with two guards, neither of whom has a defensive man, and two forwards with defenders. The defensive forward on the ball side is told to overplay his man and the offside forward to loosen up and help until the ball-side offensive forward gets the ball. At that time, the defensive help is taken off and they play one-on-one. If the ball-side forward cannot get a shot, he must throw the ball back out to his guard who reverses it to the other guard who attempts to make the penetration to his forward who, by this time, is being overplayed by his defender. This drill teaches the forwards to get open and gives them some one-on-one experience from their position. If the defense stops the offense, they change assignments.

NOTE: This drill can also be used to teach the fast break. This is done by telling the two defenders on the forwards that if they steal the ball or rebound a missed shot, they should make an outlet pass to the guard on their side of the court. The guard then dribbles to the middle, the two men who were

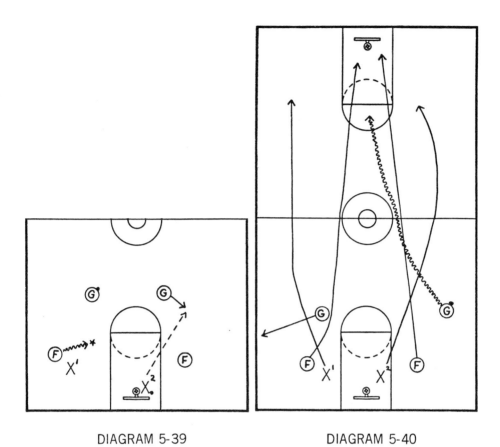

DIAGRAM 5-39   DIAGRAM 5-40

on defense fill the outside lanes, and the two former offensive forwards hustle back on defense. (Diagrams 5-39 and 5-40) The other guard drops out of the play.

The California Drill

This drill is discussed in chapter 2.

6

The Headhunter Shuffle

THE HEADHUNTER SHUFFLE VERSUS MAN-TO-MAN

The Headhunter Shuffle is a forward-oriented offense that provides either a quick shot or the opportunity to probe the defense by Shuffling.

It is a high-percentage offense because most of the shot options are in the ten- to fifteen-foot range.

The Inside Headhunter Play

This play is keyed by guard (1) passing to his forward (3) (who was Stacked with the post man (5)) and cutting diagonally toward the defender of the offside forward (4). (Diagram 6-1)

From here three options are immediately possible:

A. Player (3) may have rubbed his defender off on the post and may have a jump shot.
B. The post man rolls to the low-post position for a possible one-on-one play.
C. The offside forward (4) may have been sprung open on the Headhunter screen set by guard (1). The instructions given to (3) and (4) are that if (3) thinks (4) is wide open, he should hit him. Player (4) knows that if he receives a pass from (3) he is open, so he is to go up with a jump shot

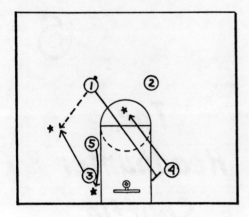

DIAGRAM 6-1

immediately. If none of these three options is open, player (3) may do one of the following.

A. Pass to guard (2) at the head of the key who reverses the ball to guard (1). (Diagram 6-2)

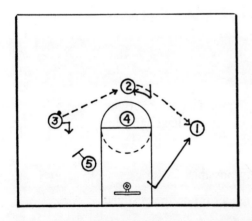

DIAGRAM 6-2

As soon as guard (1) receives the ball, forward (3) changes direction and makes a cut low off the post man (5) into the ball-side low-post area. (Diagram 6-3)

If (3) is not open, player (4), the forward at the free-throw line, comes down and screens for the post man (5) who uses the screen and swings to the ball side. (Diagram 6-4)

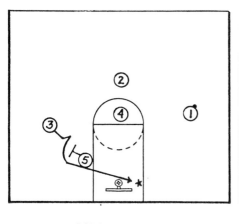

DIAGRAM 6-3

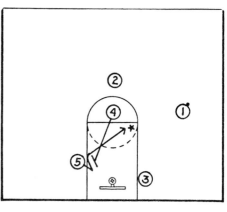

DIAGRAM 6-4

If no one is open, (1) dribbles up front and the players are back in alignment to start over with forward (3) Stacked inside the post man (5). (Diagram 6-5)

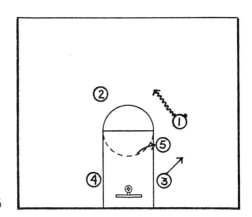

DIAGRAM 6-5

B. Pass to the post man (5) and screen for forward (4). (Diagram 6-6)

After the screen for (4), (3) rolls to the basket. The defensive guard (X¹) has been cleared by the Headhunting guard who drifted to an area on the offside of the foul lane and as high as the foul line. (Diagram 6-6)

171

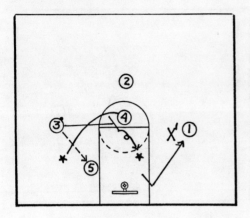

DIAGRAM 6-6

The Outside Headhunter Play

At times when the guard (1) passes to the forward stepping out of the Stack, he will take an outside cut. When this happens, forward (3) will return the ball to him and become the Headhunter himself by moving diagonally across the lane to screen for forward (4). (Diagrams 6-7 and 6-8)

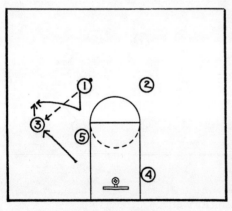

DIAGRAM 6-7

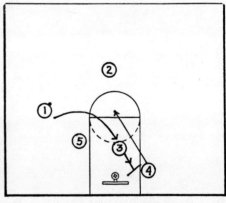

DIAGRAM 6-8

The team is now ready to run the same options with different men in the positions. (Diagrams 6-9 and 6-10)

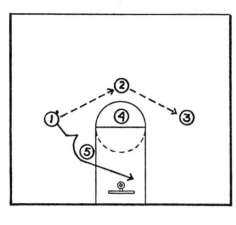

DIAGRAM 6-9

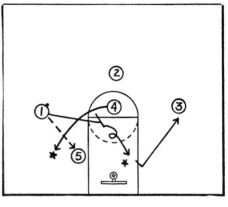

DIAGRAM 6-10

The Post Play

When a pass is made from a guard directly to the post man (5), the ball-side forward attempts to backdoor his defender. (Diagram 6-11)

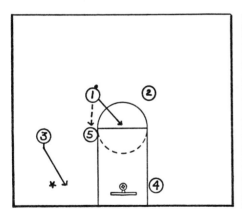

DIAGRAM 6-11

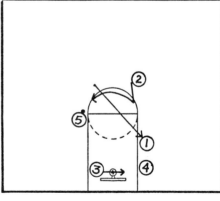

DIAGRAM 6-12

In Diagram 6-12 guard (1) crosses in front of guard (2) who changes direction and uses (1)'s moving screen to lose his man and cuts toward the post man. Guard (1) continues to form a

173

double screen with offside forward (4) for (3) who continues his backdoor cut.

The post man (5) dribbles once or twice toward the center of the free-throw line and may do one of the following.

A. Hand off to guard (2) who has lost his man on guard (1). (Diagram 6-13)

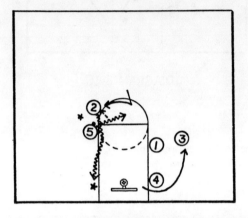

DIAGRAM 6-13

B. Or pass to the forward behind the double screen. (Diagram 6-14)

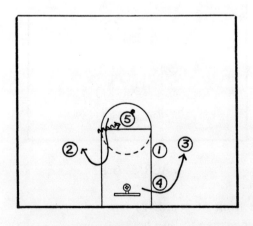

DIAGRAM 6-14

174

THE HEADHUNTER SHUFFLE AUXILIARY PLAYS

The Post Play

Another variation that may be used after a pass to the post is to again have the forward (1) on that side backdoor as before for the first option. The guard who initiated the play makes his diagonal cut and screens for the offside forward (4) who breaks to the free-throw line area looking for a pass from the post man (5). (Diagram 6-15)

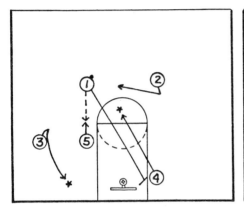

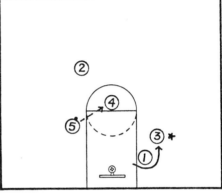

DIAGRAM 6-15   DIAGRAM 6-16

If (4) receives the ball from the post man (5) and does not have a shot, he looks for (3) who has lost his man on (1) and has a short jump shot. (Diagram 6-16)

It is up to (3) to time his cut around (1) so that he will not get there too soon. Also, the pass to the post and the clear-out by (3) give the post plenty of room for a one-on-one play.

The Lob Play

The Stacking forward (3) comes out and receives a pass from guard (1). The offside forward (4) cuts to the high post early and screens for (1) who gets a cross-court lob pass from (3). (Diagram 6-17)

175

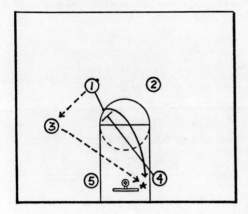

DIAGRAM 6-17

In the event this play does not work, the same options may be run.

The Lob Play from the Outside Cut

When this play is run, guard (1) passes to forward (3) and makes an outside cut as per the outside Headhunter play. Player (4) again cuts to the high-post area prematurely. Player (3) hands off to (1) and rubs his man off on (4) for a cross-court lob pass from (1). (Diagram 6-18)

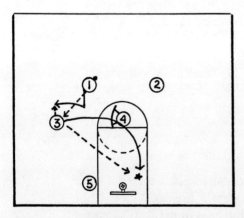

DIAGRAM 6-18

If this move fails, the same options prevail as if the outside Headhunter had been run.

The Shallow Cut Play

Ordinarily when (1) passes to (3), he makes a diagonal cut and screens for the offside forward (4). This play is keyed when (1) makes a shallow cut and comes back out front. Forward (4) moves to the ball side of the foul lane, foul line high. The offside guard (2) moves toward the ball. (Diagram 6-19)

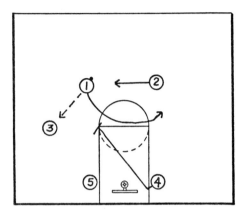

DIAGRAM 6-19

Forward (3) passes to the post man (5) and cuts over (4) and down the middle of the lane. Guard (2) uses (3) and splits off (4) with him ((3) goes first). The post man (5) may shoot, or pass to (3) down the lane or (2) for a jump shot. (Diagram 6-20)

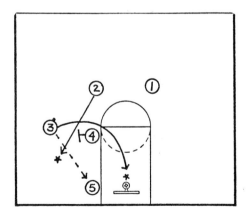

DIAGRAM 6-20

177

The Forward Low Play

After a while, the defender on the offside forward begins to anticipate the diagonal Headhunter screen. When this happens, the forward low play may be run. When guard (1) passes to his forward (3) and makes his diagonal cut to make his Headhunter screen on (4), (4)'s defender sees it coming and gets over it early.

To counter this, forward (4) moves across the lane low. (Diagram 6-21) If (4) is open, (3) passes to him. If not, forward (3) passes to the post man (5) and pinches in for forward (4) who comes around for a jump shot. (Diagram 6-22)

NOTE: It helps if the post man (5) sets up higher than usual.

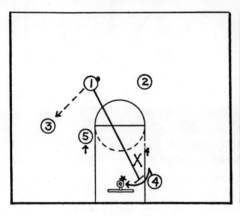

DIAGRAM 6-21

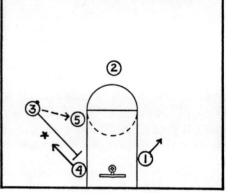

DIAGRAM 6-22

THE HEADHUNTER SHUFFLE VERSUS ZONE DEFENSES

The Basic Play

When guard (1) passes to his forward (3) and cuts through for his Headhunter screen, forward (4) cuts to the high-post area. If (3) can get the ball to him, he does. (Diagram 6-23) The penetrating guard (1) is instructed to stay in the low-post area when forward (4) receives the ball. Forward (4) then turns toward the basket for

178

a potential jump shot. When forward (4) turns, he also looks for the post man (5) who is inside of the defensive wing man on his side and the guard (1) who penetrated and made the Headhunter screen. (Diagram 6-24)

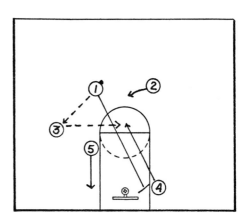

DIAGRAM 6-23

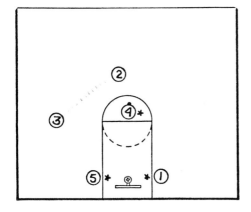

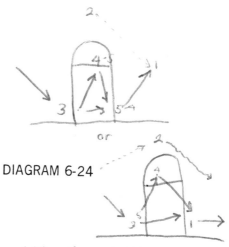

DIAGRAM 6-24

Catching the Overshift

If forward (3) cannot get the ball to forward (4) or the post man (5) for a one-on-one play, he reverses it by way of guard (2) to guard (1). Guard (1)'s rule is to stay in the low-post area until the ball is passed to the front man. Then he breaks out to the foul line extended and receives a pass from guard (2). This move may

179

catch the zone overshifted. As soon as (1) receives the pass, the offside forward cuts off the post man (5) to the ball side. (Diagram 6-25)

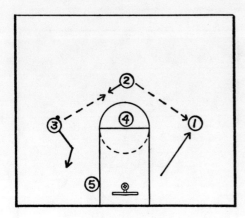

DIAGRAM 6-25

Switching the Overload

When (3) cuts across the lane, he hesitates in the ball-side low-post area and then continues to the ball-side corner. (Diagram 6-26) Forward (4) then comes down and exchanges with the post man (5) who cuts to the ball-side midpost area. (Diagram 6-27) This move results in an overload of the ball side.

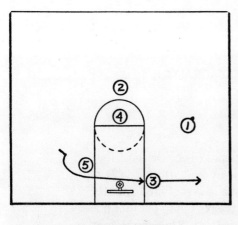

DIAGRAM 6-26

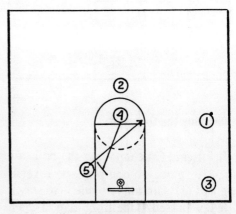

DIAGRAM 6-27

Utilizing Triangles

This move by the post man (5) and forward (4) is not particularly functional against a zone, but it puts the players back in their original positions. Guard (1) may move the ball around the triangles. If he decides to repeat the continuity, he dribbles out front. (Diagrams 6-28 and 6-29)

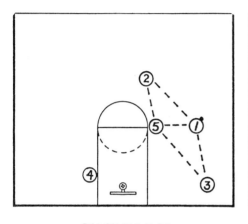 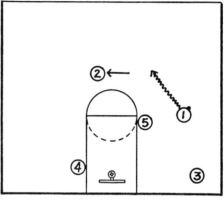

DIAGRAM 6-28   DIAGRAM 6-29

Thus, by this simple pattern, the zone has been overloaded, over-shifted, and penetrated by cutting players to the high-post area.

TEACHING THE HEADHUNTER SHUFFLE

Personnel

This offense is ideal for a team that has the following personnel.

Guards. At least one of the guards should be big enough to play forward and a very strong rebounder. It would help if the other guard was quick and possessed a great outside shot.

Post. The post man need not be a great scorer, but he must be an adequate ball-handler and rebounder.

181

Forwards. The forwards should be the scoring punch of the team. If their rebounding is strong, great; but if it is average, the team can still succeed.

Another type of team that could run this offense is one with forwards who are no bigger than the team's guards and an average-sized post man.

This offense starts with one of the forwards Stacked inside the post man. In the event the play is initiated on the weak side, the post man is instructed to swing to the ball side. (Diagram 6-30)

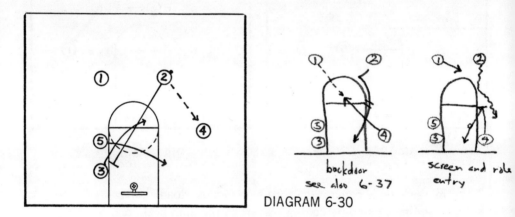

backdoor
see also 6-37

screen and role
entry

DIAGRAM 6-30

NOTE: The fact is that starting the offense on the weak side may actually be a more functional method because when the post man (5) swings to the ball side, he provides the offside forward (3) with an extra screen to use when breaking to the high-post area.

Coaching Points

The Inside Headhunter Play

When guard (1) passes to his forward and cuts diagonally to set a screen for forward (4), (4) must wait until (1) arrives before cutting to the post. Otherwise, guard (1) will be charged with moving screen. It helps if (4) gets close to his defender while (1) is cutting toward him. This makes it difficult for (X⁴) to fight through. When forward (3) receives the ball, he must pivot toward the play and simultaneously be aware of whether: (a) the offside forward utilized (1)'s screen and is open at the free-throw line, or (b) the post man (5) was able to slide down into the low-post area, off the Stack maneuver, and gain an advantage over his defender.

When the ball is passed to the offside forward (4), this means that he is open and should look for the shot. The passer is instructed not to make this pass unless the cutter is definitely open. (Diagram 6-31)

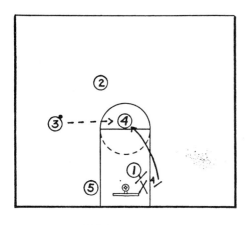

DIAGRAM 6-31   DIAGRAM 6-32

When the ball is passed to the post man (5), the offside forward (4), who cut to the free-throw line, must wait for the screen and not be moving when (3) screens his man. It would help if (4) would fake toward the basket before coming off the screen. If his defender would not back up and respect this move to the basket, (4) should cut and call for the ball. (Diagram 6-32)

If (4)'s defender reacts to the fake, it will set him up for the screen by (3). After (3) screens, he should roll to the basket and keep his eye on the ball as much as possible. (Diagram 6-33)

183

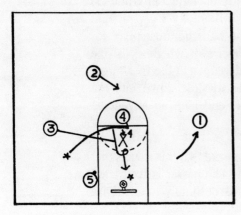

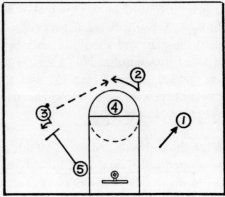

DIAGRAM 6-33   DIAGRAM 6-34

Guard (1) must clear foul line high to allow this play to work.

If neither of these initial options is open, the Shuffle is run. Timing the initiation of this phase of the offense is up to guard (2) in Diagram 6-34, who must stay clear and keep his man busy until (3) has explored the first two options. When this has been done, (2) must change direction, cut toward (3), and receive the ball at the middle of the head of the key. This is a dangerous pass unless (2) times his cut perfectly. It helps somewhat if a bounce pass is used.

When this pass is made, the post man (5) must step up into (3)'s man. Player (3) changes direction and cuts low off of the post man as the ball is passed from (2) to (1). This fact must be stressed: *(3) should not cut until (1) has the ball and is ready to pass to him.* Player (3) should expect to get the pass basket high. This means that if (3) cuts and beats his man and (1) is slow in getting the ball to him, (3) should slow down and spread out to maintain his advantage over his defender. It should also be pointed out that three seconds is measured by a count of one-thousand-one, one-thousand-two, one-thousand-three. (Diagram 6-35)

At this point the reason for the post man's stepping into (3)'s

184

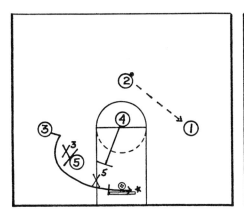

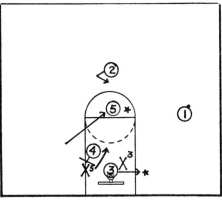

DIAGRAM 6-35   DIAGRAM 6-36

defender becomes apparent. If (5) has impeded (X^3)'s progress, his defender (X^5) must help until (X^3) recovers. This sets up (X^5) for the second phase of the Shuffle when (4) comes down to screen him and often results in an unmolested jump shot for the post man (5) at the free-throw line. (Diagram 6-36)

The Outside Headhunter Play

This is the same play with the assignments changed, so the same coaching points prevail.

The Post Play

When starting the post play, it is important for guard (1) to first fake to his forward (3) and then pass to the post man (5). This sets up (3)'s backdoor cut. At times, we have keyed this play with a fake underhand pass. Again, a bounce pass is preferred from (1) to the post man (5). Forward (3) pushes off his front outside foot and goes behind his defender as the bounce pass hits the floor. (Diagram 6-37)

The post man (5) may now pass to (2) splitting off (1) or take two dribbles and pass to (3) behind the double screen set by (1) and (4). (Diagram 6-38)

185

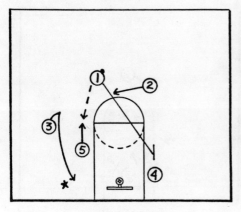

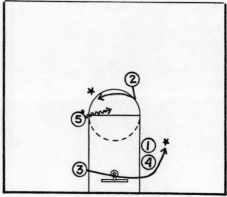

DIAGRAM 6-37   DIAGRAM 6-38

DRILLS TO TEACH THE HEADHUNTER SHUFFLE

High-Post Jump Shot

The player in the onside guard position (1) initiates the drill by passing to (3) in the onside forward position. Player (1) makes the diagonal screen for (2) in the offside forward position, who comes up and takes a jump shot after receiving a pass for (3). (Diagram 6-39) After the shot, (1) rebounds and throws out to (4) who is the next man in the onside guard position. Player (2) replaces (3), (3) goes to the end of the guard line, and the same play may now be repeated. (Diagram 6-40)

The Split Drill

Player (1) is the first man in the guard line. He passes to the onside forward (3), screens horizontally for (2), and bounces out to clear the area under the basket. Player (2) uses (1)'s screen and comes to the high-post area. Player (3) receives the pass from (1), and passes to the post man (7). Player (7) sets up in the post. (Diagram 6-41)

Player (1) stays clear to give (3) room to roll; (2) receives (3)'s screen and comes to the ball; (3) screens and rolls to the area

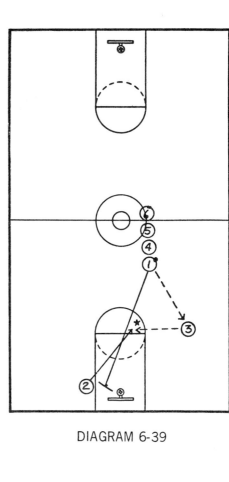

DIAGRAM 6-39

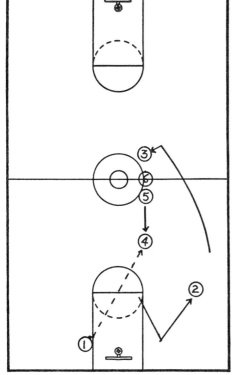

DIAGRAM 6-40

187

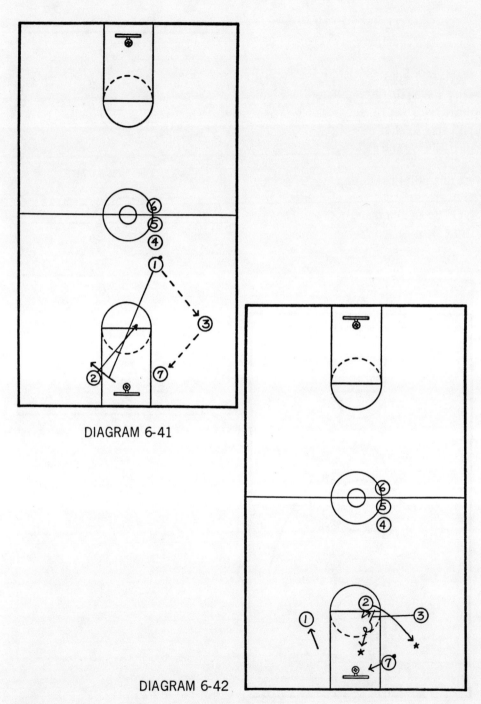

DIAGRAM 6-41

DIAGRAM 6-42

vacated by (1); and (7) passes to either (3) or (2) and turns to rebound. (Diagram 6-42)

Player (1) goes to (2)'s starting position; (2) replaces (3); (3), after his split, goes to the far sideline, makes an outlet pass throwing it to (4), and goes to the end of the guard line. Player (4) prepares to start a new sequence; (7) rebounds, makes an outlet pass to (3), and returns to his original position. (Diagram 6-43)

At this point begin a new sequence. (Diagram 6-44)

NOTE: In Diagram 6-43, either (7), (1), or (2) may rebound, but (3) must get to the sideline for an outlet pass.

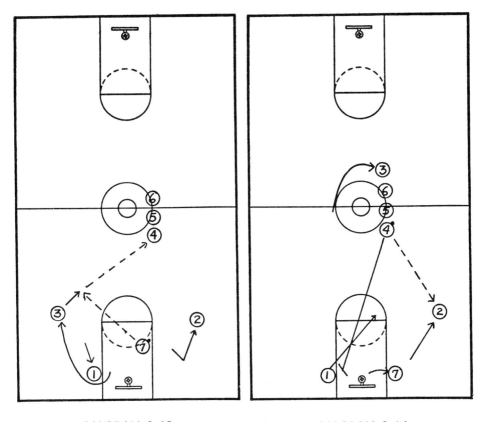

DIAGRAM 6-43   DIAGRAM 6-44

✱ The Shuffle Phase Drill

As shown in Diagrams 6-45 and 6-46, the Shuffle is turned over twice. When the ball gets to the second side, (3) may pass to either (4) for a layup shot or (1) for a jump shot at the free-throw line.

NOTE: After the drill has been run, players (1), (2), (3), and (4) are replaced, but the feeder (F) stays the same.

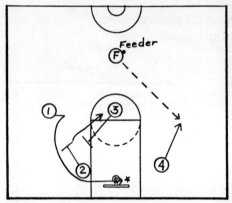 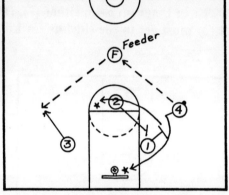

DIAGRAM 6-45   DIAGRAM 6-46

7

The Stack and Shuffle Continuity

THE STACK AND SHUFFLE CONTINUITY VERSUS MAN-TO-MAN

Two of the most popular offensive techniques are the Shuffle and the Stack. The following offense combines the two techniques and allows a team to use them both during a given offensive series.

The Basic Stack Play

Since the offense starts from a point guard and double Stack formation, the Stack Continuity will be covered first. As shown in Diagram 7-1, the point guard (1) picks up his dribble and both bottom men, (2) and (3), on the Stack step-out. When the point man (1) passes to a wing man (2), he screens opposite for the other wing man (3).

The wing man with the ball (2) may now (a) jump shoot, (b) pass to the post (4), or (c) pass to the new man (3), at the point. When the wing man (2) chooses to pass inside, he splits the post with the point man. (Diagram 7-2)

In that case, (1) is the back man and is responsible for defensive balance. When the ball is passed back to the point, the continuity

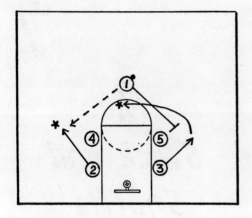

DIAGRAM 7-1

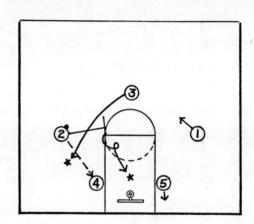

DIAGRAM 7-2

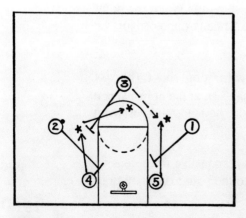

DIAGRAM 7-3

192

goes on. (Diagram 7-3) Player (3) will pass to a new wing man and screen opposite for the other.

The Basic Shuffle Play

The Shuffle play starts from the same formation. After the wing men step out, the ball is passed to one of them, (2). The offside post man (5) comes to the ball side to form a double screen with the post man on that side. (Diagram 7-4) The point man (1) makes the same screen opposite he did in the Stack phase and the offside wing man (3) cuts to the head of the key as before. (Diagram 7-4)

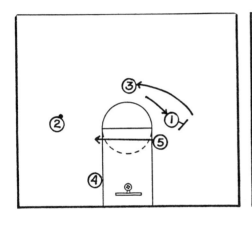

DIAGRAM 7-4

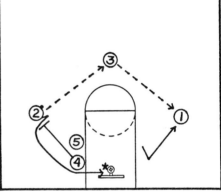

DIAGRAM 7-5

From here, the Shuffle action takes place. Player (2) reverses the ball to (1) by way of (3), and then cuts low off the double screen formed by (5) and (4). To help (2) get open, the bottom man (4) on the double screen steps out and makes a definite screen on the defender of (2). (Diagram 7-5)

Player (1) attempts to get the ball to (2) basket high. If (2) is not open, the point man (3) screens opposite for the now wing man (4) who comes out front for a possible jump shot. If he receives the ball and has no shot, the continuity goes on. *Again, the key man is the offside post man.* (A) *If he comes to the ball side* the Shuffle is in order. (Diagrams 7-6 and 7-7)

193

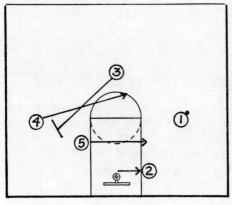 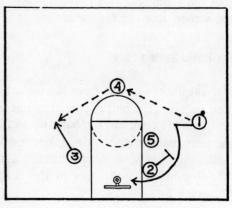

DIAGRAM 7-6   From shuffle
to shuffle   DIAGRAM 7-7

(B) If the offside post man (5) decides to slide down instead of coming across, the offense has converted to the Stack phase. (Diagrams 7-8 and 7-9)

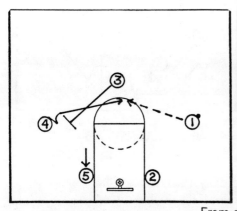 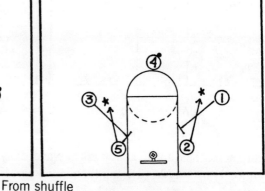

DIAGRAM 7-8   From shuffle
to stack   DIAGRAM 7-9

CONVERSION

Diagrams 7-10 through 7-15 show the offense being run continuously with the offside post man selecting the phase.

Starts in Stacks. (Diagram 7-10)

Player (1) runs the Stack options. (Diagram 7-11)

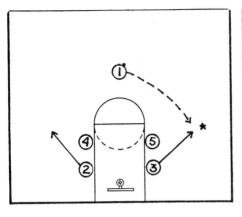

DIAGRAM 7-10

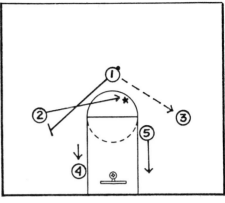

DIAGRAM 7-11

Player (4) slides down and doesn't come to ball side so the offense stays in the Stack phase. (Diagram 7-12)

Player (3) calls the Shuffle by coming to the ball side to form the double screen with (1). (Diagram 7-13)

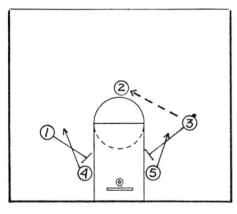

DIAGRAM 7-12

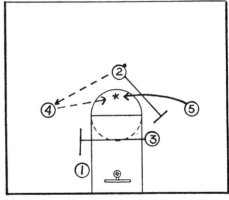

DIAGRAM 7-13

The two Shuffle options are run. Player (2) may pass to (4) coming under the double screen set by (1) and (3) or to (1) at the head of the key who, after screening for (4), used (5)'s screen to get open. (Diagram 7-14)

195

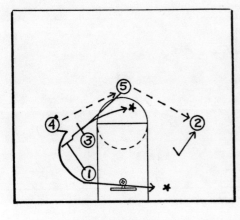

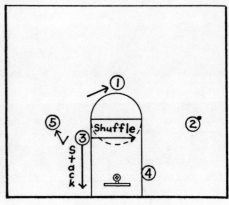

DIAGRAM 7-14   DIAGRAM 7-15

If (3) comes across, the Shuffle continues; if he slides down, the offense goes back to the Stack phase. (Diagram 7-15)

AUXILIARY PLAYS FOR THE STACK AND SHUFFLE CONTINUITY

When a team plays a disciplined pattern such as the Stack and Shuffle Continuity, the defense will usually begin to anticipate and overplay the scoring options. To combat this defensive ploy, a team running this sort of offense must have pressure-relievers. These are offensive options that allow a team to break away from their regular patterns by way of a different scoring option and then return to their pattern when the pressure-reliever is over.

The High-Post Screen

In Diagram 7-16, the team has moved in to their Shuffle set and are prepared to run it. The problem arises when the defender on (3) will not allow him to get the ball.

Player (4) calls this high-post screen by clearing to the corner. This tells (5) to go blind screen the point man's defender. Player (2) passes to (4) in the corner and (3) cuts off (5) and to the basket; (5) rolls after setting the screen; (1) comes to the point position to clear his man. (Diagram 7-17)

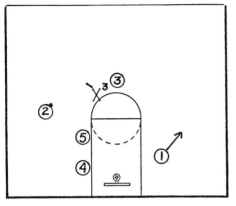

DIAGRAM 7-16

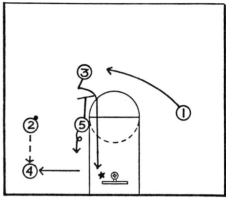

DIAGRAM 7-17

If neither (3) nor (5) is open, (2) cuts through on a diagonal type cut and clears to the far side of the court. Player (5) steps out into (4)'s defensive man and they work a screen-and-roll play. (Diagram 7-18)

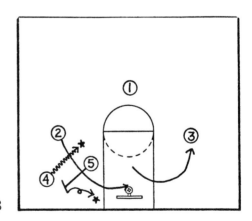

DIAGRAM 7-18

From here, if a shot has not developed, the team can return to either the Shuffle or the Stack phase. The key player is (3), the offside high man.

If, as the ball is passed to the point man, (3) comes across the lane, it reverts the team to the Shuffle set. (Diagrams 7-19 and 7-20)

197

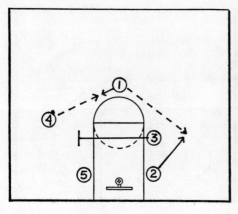

DIAGRAM 7-19

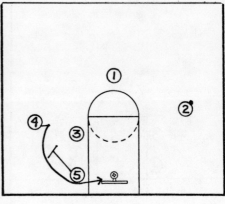

DIAGRAM 7-20

If (3) chooses not to come across the lane, the Stack phase of the offense will be run. (Diagrams 7-21 and 7-22)

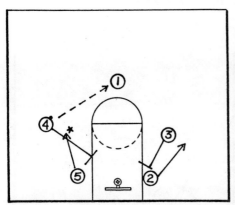

DIAGRAM 7-21

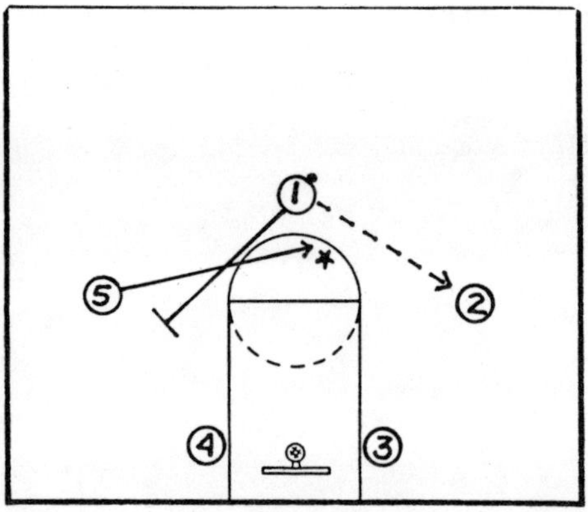

DIAGRAM 7-22

The Backdoor Play

Another way to combat pressure on the point man is the backdoor play. In Diagram 7-23, (3) is being overplayed and cannot receive the ball from (2).

The offside wing man breaks to the high post inside of (3), receives a bounce pass from (2), and looks for (3) on his back-

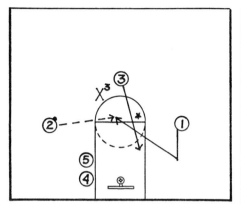

DIAGRAM 7-23

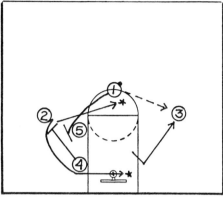

DIAGRAM 7-24

door cut. If (3) is not open, he cuts sharply to the side of the lane, free-throw line high, and receives a pass from (3) and the Shuffle continues. (Diagram 7-24)

To return the team to the Stack phase, (1) must hold the ball and not relay it to (3). Player (2) sees this is being done, butts to the other side, and the double Stack is formed. (Diagram 7-25)

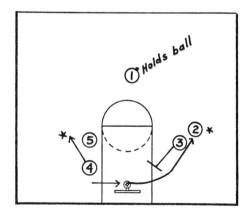

DIAGRAM 7-25

The Low-Post Split

In this sequence, the ball is passed to player (4) in the low-post area after the offside high post has cut to the ball side. (Diagram 7-26)

199

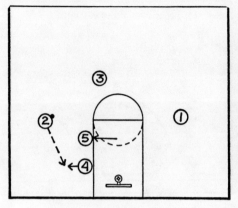

DIAGRAM 7-26

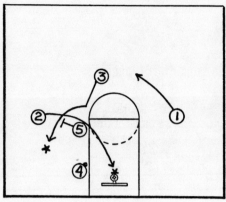

DIAGRAM 7-27

When this happens, wing man (2) splits the post with the point man (3) and utilizes the high-post man to get open. (Diagram 7-27)

NOTE: Player (1) must go to the point to clear his man.

If (3), who is the primary option on this play, receives the ball from (4) off the split and has no shot, he may revert back to the Shuffle action by passing out to (1) who will, in turn, reverse the ball to (2). (Diagram 7-28)

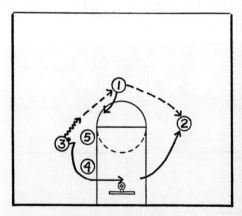

DIAGRAM 7-28

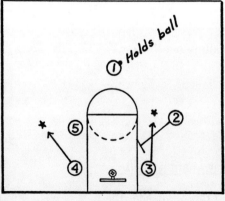

DIAGRAM 7-29

If (1) chooses to revert to the Stack, he will hold the ball and wait for (3) to go to the opposite side to form the double Stack. (Diagram 7-29)

The Wing Clear (from the Double Stack)

After both wings have cut off their respective post men, the point man finds he can get the ball to neither of them. Seeing this, wing man (2) clears out and goes to the opposite side of the court. (Diagram 7-30)

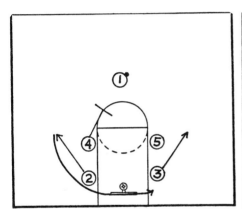

DIAGRAM 7-30

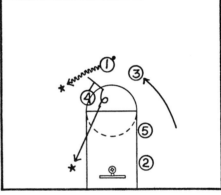

DIAGRAM 7-31

As (2) clears, he lets the post man on his side (4) know by calling out "Clear." This tells (4) to step up and play two-on-two with (1). The offside wing man (3) goes to the point for defensive balance. (Diagram 7-31)

If neither (1) nor (4) is open on the screen-and-roll play that developed, (1) passes out to (3). From here, the next play will be determined by the offside high man (5). If he comes across, the team will Shuffle. (Diagram 7-32)

If (5) does not come across, the Stack play is in order. (Diagram 7-33)

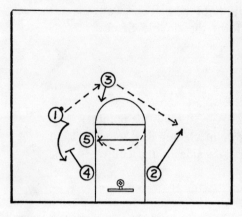

DIAGRAM 7-32

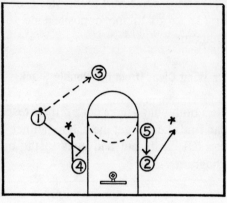

DIAGRAM 7-33

THE STACK AND SHUFFLE CONTINUITY VERSUS ZONE DEFENSES

When using this offense against zone defenses, the same two patterns are run with some minor adjustments.

The Stack Phase

When running either the Stack or Shuffle phase, the pick opposite is not a functional move against zone defense, so when point man (1) passes to a wing man (as to wing man (2) in Diagram 7-34), he now cuts down and through the zone.

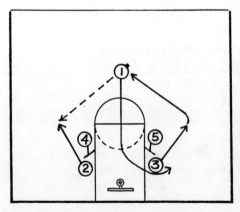

DIAGRAM 7-34

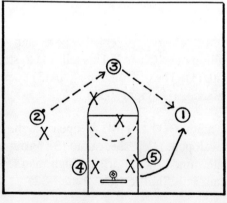

DIAGRAM 7-35

As before, he is now replaced at the point by the offside wing man (3). This opens up the possibility of (2) reversing the ball by way of (3) to (1) and catching the zone overshifted. Post man (5) may assist cutter (1) in getting open by screening the overshifted zone and not allowing it to come out after (1). (Diagram 7-35)

When the opposition becomes too aware of this reverse move, the new point man (3) may fake the reverse pass to (2) and cause the zone to hurriedly shift in that direction. This will open up (4) coming off a screen set by (2) from the wing position. (Diagram 7-36)

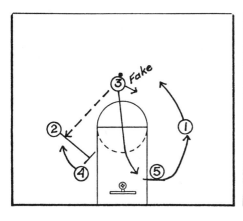

DIAGRAM 7-36

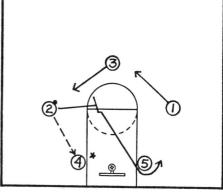

DIAGRAM 7-37

If this doesn't work, (3) makes the point man's cut down and through the zone to the weak side. Player (1) replaces him at the point. (Diagram 7-37)

If wing man (2) would have chosen to pass to the post man after receiving the ball from (1), the split play would be run. After (2) screened for the new point man (3), he would go through the zone and out on the weak side. (Diagram 7-37) Post man (4) may now shoot if he is open, or pass to (3) who has found a hole in the perimeter of the zone. If (3) is not open, he may reverse the ball to (2) by way of (1) who has taken the point. (Diagram 7-38)

The offside post man (5) again aids this play. He traps the zone

203

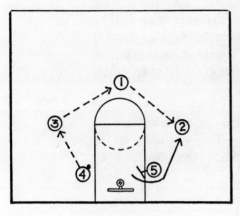

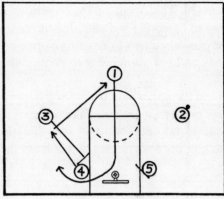

DIAGRAM 7-38   DIAGRAM 7-39

inside by screening and not permitting the nearest zone player to get back to (2). After the ball is reversed to (2), the continuity would be maintained by (1) cutting through the zone and being replaced by (4) at the point. (Diagram 7-39)

The Shuffle Phase

To repeat, the Shuffle phase starts in the same manner as the Stack phase and is called when the offside post man cuts to the ball side as shown by player (5) in Diagram 7-40.

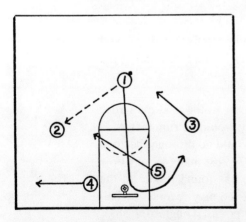

DIAGRAM 7-40

NOTE: Against zones, point man (1) again cuts down and through the zone instead of screening opposite.

When (5) makes this cut against zones, it keys (4) to swing to the ball-side corner and overload that side. The man with the ball (2) may now: (a) utilize the overload triangle created by players (4), (5), and himself; or (b) reverse the ball to (1) on the weak side, which would set the Shuffle cut in motion. As (1) receives the ball, (2) makes his cut through the zone, (3) goes down and through the zone to the weak side, and (4) goes out front. (Diagrams 7-41 and 7-42)

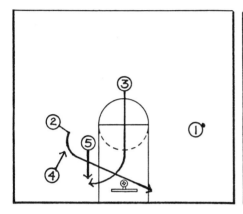 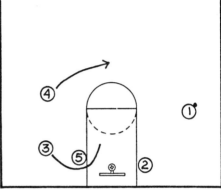

DIAGRAM 7-41   DIAGRAM 7-42

Using this offense against zone defenses at first appears to be very complicated. Upon further examination, it simply utilizes the same cuts and keys as used against man-to-man defenses with one exception. When the point man reverses the ball from wing to wing, he cuts down and through the zone instead of passing and screening opposite.

TEACHING THE STACK AND SHUFFLE CONTINUITY

Personnel

This offense has a one-man front. This means that you must have a point man who can bring the ball up the court under pressure and initiate the plays. The strength of this point man should be a deciding factor in choosing the other starters. If he has great talent, it is possible to start four other players who have size and may lack mobility. If you lack the great point man, you may start three small men and two big ones.

NOTE: If you have no big men, you can run this offense in order to move the big defensive man out of the pivot area.

Coaching Points

The keynote to a moving offense of this sort is, of course, timing. Also, the player in the offside post position must follow this rule: *If the wing man with the ball is tall and can post his man, don't come across; run the Stack. If he is small and mobile, the Shuffle is best, so come across and form the double screen that keys the Shuffle.*

The Stack Phase

When initiating the Stack play, the defensive men of the two men on the inside of the Stack must respect the fact that their men may go inside for a layup if they overplay them coming out of the Stack. It is a functional move to have the two inside men cross to disallow the overplay. (Diagram 7-43)

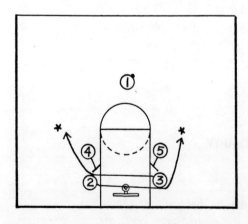

DIAGRAM 7-43

This move takes the pressure off and often results in easy jump shots.

Once the ball has been thrown to one of the wing men, the point man must screen opposite for the other. This must be a Headhunter screen. It must be definite and the defender should not slide through easily. The wing man cutting off the screen can help by changing directions and not moving until the screen has been set.

The stop man on the Stack must slide down and assume a wide pivot stance. If he is overplayed, he should give the wing man a target and get some part of his body between his defender and the basket. The wing man should feed him away from the defensive man.

Above all, the offensive players must have the ability to know what options may develop and the patience to wait for them.

The Shuffle Phase

The Shuffle cutter, as shown by (2) in Diagram 7-44, must walk his defender up to the double screen and cut opposite the defensive pressure.

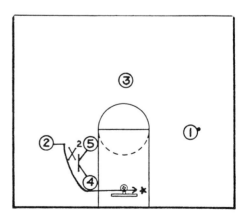

DIAGRAM 7-44

The bottom screener must be taught that if he sets a good screen, his defender will be forced to switch and he (4) will be open when he comes out front. (Diagrams 7-45 and 7-46)

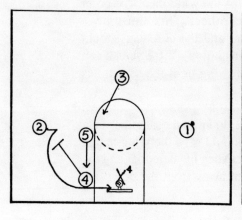

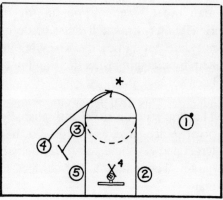

DIAGRAM 7-45   DIAGRAM 7-46

DRILLS TO TEACH THE STACK AND SHUFFLE CONTINUITY

The Recognition Drill

The players who run this offense must be able to quickly recognize which phase has been called. Players are placed in the positions with no defenders. The ball is then given to a wing man. As the wing man (2) passes the ball to the point, the offside wing man will either start across or slide down. The wing man who started the action must then make the proper response of either cutting off the double screen or pinching in to screen for the low-post man.

The Skeleton Drill

This is merely running the plays over and over with no defense. Some coaches use music to stress the timing factor. After a while, a passive defense may be added.

The California Drill

This drill was previously explained in chapter 2. It teaches the players timing and how to cut off an offside screen.

208

The Defensive Balance Drill

The offense is run with a defense. When the defense acquires the ball, they are told to fast break. Two of the weaknesses of moving offenses are: (a) it is difficult to decide who has primary defensive responsibility and (b) who are the primary offensive rebounders. This drill should be run often and it should be stressed that the point man is the first man back on defense followed by the offside wing man. The other three men must charge the offensive board.

Index

A

Auxiliary plays:
    Four-Man Passing Game, 24-33
    Headhunter Shuffle, 175-178
    High-Post Wall, 111-128
    Multi-Option Continuity, 153-158
    Passing Game Shuffle, 64-69
    Post-Oriented Stack, 90-93
    Stack and Shuffle Continuity, 196-202

B

Backdoor plays:
    drill, 105
    Four-Man Passing Game, 26-28
    Passing Game Shuffle, 64-65, 76-77
    Post-Oriented Stack, 92-93, 101-102
    Stack and Shuffle Continuity, 198-199
Breakdown drill, 143

C

California drill, **80-81**, 167, 208
Catching the overshift, 179-180
Continuities, Passing Game, 33-41 (see also Four-Man Passing Game)
Conversion, 194-196
Corner play, 155-156
Corner-reverse play, 113-116
Cross-court lob play, 153-155
Cross-cut play, 44-46
Cross drill, 103
Cross, High-Post Wall, 127-128
Cross play, High-Post Wall, 110-111, 137, 143
Crossing action, 98-99
Cutting off:
    low post, 46-47
    post man, 163-164

Cutting tempo, 50
Cutting through the zone:
    Four-Man Passing Game, 44
    Passing Game Shuffle, 72-73

D

David Thompson play, 100
Defensive balance drill, 209
Double-cross continuity, 40-41
Double-cut series, 119-123
Double-inside screen, 28-29
Double-post-stack Passing Game continuity, 37-38
Dribble-chase against a zone, 47-48
Dribble-chase rule, 25-26
Drills:
    backdoor, 105
    breakdown, 143
    California, 80-81, 167, 208
    cross, 103
    defensive balance, 209
    forwards' two-on-two, 166-167
    Headhunter Shuffle, 186-190
    high-post jump shot, 186
    High-Post Wall Offense, 143-145
    isolation, 145
    Multi-Option Continuity, 165-167
    offensive, progressive sequence, 83
    offside screen-and-roll, 79-80
    one-on-one in post, 165-166
    Passing Game, 51-56
    Passing Game Shuffle, 78-83
    Post-Oriented Stack Offense, 103-105
    recognition, 143, 208
    screen-and-roll, 78
    shadow, from corner position, 55
    shadow, from side position, 54-55
    Shuffle Phase, 190

Drills: *(cont.)*
    skeleton, 208
    split, 105, 186, 188, 189
    Stack, 103
    Stack and Shuffle Continuity, 208-209
    strongside recognition, 81-82
    three-man shadow, 51-54
    three-on-three (live), 56
    three-times-around, 145

E

Exchange-switch play, 32

F

Forward-across play, 31-32
Forward fake, 112-113
Forward low play, 178
Forwards, 151, 162, 182
Forwards' two-on-two, 166-167
Four-Man Passing Game:
    against zone defenses, 41-50
        cross-cut play, 44-46
        cutting off low post, 46-47
        cutting through zone, 44
        dribble-chase against zone, 47-49
        overloading and overshifting, 44-47
        passing and cutting tempo, 50
        quick cut, 44
        rotating zone players, 47-49
        screening zone, 49-50
        splitting defensive perimeter, 42-44
        versus even front zone, 43-44
        versus odd front zone, 42-43
    auxiliary plays, 24-33
        backdoor play, 26-28
        double-inside screen, 28-29
        dribble-chase rule, 25-26
        exchange-switch play, 32
        forward-across play, 31-32
        over-the-top play, 32-33
        post-opposite play, 30-31
        quick-cut play, 24-25
        second-guard-through play, 26
        Stack, 30
    continuities, 33-41
        double-cross, 40-41
        double-post-stack Passing Game, 37-38
        reverse-action-type, 34-35
        Shuffle-type action, 39-40
        slashing-type, 35-36

Four-Man Passing Game: *(cont.)*
    shadow drill from corner position, 50
    shadow drill from side position, 54-55
    teaching offense, 50-51
        coaching points, 50-51
        personnel, 50
    three-man shadow drill, 51-54
        back, 54
        behind, 53
        over, 52
        through, 52-53
    three-on-three live, 56
    versus man-to-man, 15-24
        basic movement, 16
        basic movement rules, 16-21
        cutting to basket, 19-21
        high post, 21
        offside post, 21-22
        onside post, 21
        pass ball and move away from your pass, 16-18
        pivot man, 21
        roaming post, 22-24
        utilization of pivot man, 18-19

G

Guards, 150-151, 162, 181
Guards' crossing action, Multi-Option Continuity, 165

H

Headhunter Shuffle:
    auxiliary plays, 175-178
        forward low, 178
        lob, 175-176
        lob from outside cut, 176
        post, 175
        shallow cut, 177
    drills, 186-190
        high-post jump shot, 186
        Shuffle phase, 190
        split, 186-189
    teaching, 181-186
        coaching points, 182-185
        forwards, 182
        guards, 181
        inside Headhunter play, 182-183
        outside Headhunter play, 185
        personnel, 181-182
        post, 181
        post play, 185

Headhunter Shuffle: *(cont.)*
  versus man-to-man, 169-174
    inside Headhunter play, 169-172
    outside Headhunter play, 172-173
    post play, 173-174
  versus zone defenses, 178-181
    basic play, 178-179
    catching the overshift, 179-180
    switching the overload, 180
    utilizing triangles, 181
High-post jump shot, 186
High post, pivot man, 21
High-post screen, 196-198
High-Post Wall:
  auxiliary plays, 111-128
    corner-reverse play, 113-116
    cross, 127-128
    double-cut series, 119-123
    double-cut series against zone defenses, 121-122
    forward fake, 112-113
    inside cut, 125-126
    Kas's play, 111-112
    offside post rotation, 121
    outside cut, 126-127
    overload variation, 122-123
    post-opposite play, 118-119
    Shuffle phase, 123-128
    three-in-a-row play, 116-118
  drills, 143-145
    breakdown, 143
    isolation, 145
    recognition, 143
    three-times-around, 145
  teaching, 138-143
    coaching points, 138
    cross play, 143
    initial spacing, 138
    inside-cut play, 139-140
    outside cut, 140-142
    personnel, 138
    reverse pivot, 139-140
    straight backdoor, 139
  versus man-to-man, 107-111
    cross play, 110-111
    inside cut, 107-108
    outside cut, 108-110
  versus zone defenses, 129-137
    cross play, 137
    inside-cut play, 131-134
    outside-cut play, 134-137
    splitting the zone, 128-130

I

Inside cut, 107-108, 125-126, 131-134, 139-140
Inside Headhunter play, 169-172, 182-183
Isolation drill, 145

K

Kas's play, 111-112

L

Lob play, 175-176
Low-post split play:
  Post-Oriented Stack Offense, 102-103
  Stack and Shuffle Continuity, 199-201

M

Man-to-man:
  Four-Man Passing Game versus, 15-24
  Headhunter Shuffle versus, 169-174
  High-Post Wall versus, 107-111
  Multi-Option Continuity versus, 147-152
  Passing Game Shuffle versus, 57-64
  Post-Oriented Stack versus, 85-90
  Stack and Shuffle Continuity versus, 191-196
Moving screen, 164-165
Multi-Option Continuity:
  auxiliary plays, 153-158
    corner, 155-156
    cross-court lob, 153-155
    wall play, 156-158
  drills, 165-167
    California, 167
    forwards' two-on-two, 166-167
    one-on-one in post, 165-166
  teaching, 161-165
    coaching points, 163
    cutting off post man, 163-164
    forwards, 162
    guards, 162
    guards' crossing action, 165
    moving screen, 164-165
    personnel, 162-163
    post man, 162-163
  versus man-to-man, 147-152
    forwards, 151
    guards, 150-151

Multi-Option Continuity: *(cont.)*
    players' rules, 150-151
    post man, 151
    split rule, 151-152
    versus zone defenses, 158-161
        forward options, 159-161
        guard options, 161
        rotating front, 158-159

O

Offside post, pivot man, 21-22
Offside post rotation, 121
Offside screen-and-roll drill, 79-80
Offside screen and roll, Passing Game
    Shuffle, 74-75
One-on-one in post, 165-166
Onside post, pivot man, 21
Outside cut, 108-110, 126-127,
    134-137, 140-142
Outside Headhunter play, 172-173, 185
Over-the-top play, 32-33
Overload triangles, utilizing, 70-71
Overload variation, High-Post Wall,
    122-123
Overloading and overshifting, 44-47

P

Passing and cutting tempo, 50
Passing Game Shuffle:
    auxiliary plays, 64-69
        backdoor, 64-66
        sagger, 67-69
        second-guard-through, 66-67
    California drill, 80-81
    offside screen-and-roll drill, 79-80
    pass and screen opposite, 62-64
    pass to forward and cut through, 61-62
    progressive sequence of offensive drills,
        83
    screen-and-roll drill, 78-79
    strongside recognition drill, 81-82
    teaching, 73-78
        backdoor play, 76-77
        coaching points, 73
        offside screen and roll, 74-75
        pattern set phase, 74-75
        second-guard-through play, 77-78
        Shuffle phase, 75-76
    versus man-to-man, 57-64
        basic Shuffle, 59-61
        pattern set move, 57-58

Passing Game Shuffle: *(cont.)*
    versus zone defense, 69-73
        cutting through the zone, 72-73
        screening the zone, 71-72
        splitting the zone, 69-70
        utilizing overload triangles, 70-71
Passing set phase, 74-75
Pattern set move, 57-58
Pivot man, Four-Man Passing Game, 21-24
Post, 181
Post man, 151, 162-163
Post-opposite play, 30-31, 118-119
Post-Oriented Stack:
    auxiliary plays, 90-93
        backdoor play, 92-93
        wall play, 90-91
        wall play outside cut, 91-92
    drills, 103-105
        backdoor, 105
        cross, 103
        split, 105
        Stack, 103
    teaching, 98-103
        backdoor play, 101-102
        coaching points, 98
        crossing action, 98-99
        David Thompson play, 100
        low-post split play, 102-103
        strongside action, 103
        weakside plays, 98
    versus man-to-man, 85
        backdoor, 87-89
        split the low post, 86-87
        strongside action, 89-90
        weakside action, 85-89
    versus zone defense, 93-98
        pass to high post, 94-95
        pass to low post, 95-96
        strongside action, 97-98
        wall play, 96-97
        weakside action, 93-94
Post play, 173-174, 175, 185

Q

Quick-cut play, 24-25, 44

R

Recognition drill, 143
Reverse-action-type continuity, 34-35
Reverse pivot, 139-140

Roaming post, pivot man, 22
Rotating front, 158-159
Rotating the zone players, 47-49

S

Sagger play, Passing Game Shuffle, 67-68
Screen-and-roll drill, 78-79
Screen and roll on point guard, Passing
    Game Shuffle, 74
Screening the zone:
    Four-Man Passing Game, 49-50
    Passing Game Shuffle, 71-72
Second-guard-through play:
    Four-Man Passing Game, 26
    Passing Game Shuffle, 66-67, 77-78
Shadow drill:
    from corner position, 55
    from side position, 54-55
    three-man, 51-54
Shallow cut play, 177
Shuffle phase:
    drill, 190
    High-Post Wall auxiliary plays, 123-128
    Stack and Shuffle Continuity, 204-205,
        207-208
Shuffle play, basic, 193-194
Shuffle-type action, 39-40
Skeleton drill, 208
Slashing-type continuity, 35-36
Split drill, 105, 186-189
Split rule, Multi-Option Continuity versus
    man-to-man, 151-152
Splitting:
    defensive perimeter, 42-44
    zone, 69-70, 128-130
Stack:
    drill, Post-Oriented Stack, 103
    Four-Man Passing Game, 30
Stack and Shuffle Continuity:
    auxiliary plays, 196-202
        backdoor play, 198-199
        high-post screen, 196-198
        low-post split, 199-201
        wing clear, 201-202
    drills, 208-209
        California, 208
        defensive balance, 209
        skeleton, 208
    teaching, 205-208
        coaching points, 206

Stack and Shuffle Continuity: (cont.)
    personnel, 205-206
    Shuffle phase, 207-208
    Stack phase, 206-207
    versus man-to-man, 191-196
        basic Shuffle play, 193-194
        basic Stack play, 191-193
        conversion, 194-196
    versus zone defenses, 202-205
        Shuffle phase, 204-205
        Stack phase, 202-204
Stack phase, Stack and Shuffle Continuity,
    202-204, 206-207
Stack play, basic, 191-193
Straight backdoor, 139
Strongside action:
    Post-Oriented Stack versus man-to-
        man, 89-90
    Post-Oriented Stack versus zone de-
        fense, 97-98
    teaching Post-Oriented Stack, 103
Strongside recognition drill, 81-82
Switching the overload, 180

T

Three-in-a-row play, 116-118
Three-on-three (live), 56
Three-times-around drill, 145
Triangles, utilizing, 181

W

Wall play:
    Multi-Option Continuity, 156-158
    Post-Oriented Stack, 90-91
Weakside action:
    Post-Oriented Stack versus man-to-
        man, 85-89
    Post-Oriented Stack versus zone de-
        fense, 93-97
    teaching Post-Oriented Stack, 98-103
Wing clear, 201-202

Z

Zone defenses:
    Headhunter Shuffle versus, 178-181

Zone defenses: *(cont.)*
    High-Post Wall versus, 128-137
    Multi-Option Continuity versus,
        158-161
    Passing Game Shuffle, 69-73

Zone defenses: *(cont.)*
    Post-Oriented Stack versus, 93-98
    Stack and Shuffle Continuity versus,
        202-205
    using Passing Game against, 41-50

DATE DUE

Demco, Inc. 38-293